History & Geography 300
Teacher's Guide

CONTENTS

Author: **Alpha Omega Staff**
Editor: Alan Christopherson, M.S.

Alpha Omega Publications ®

300 North McKemy Avenue, Chandler, Arizona 85226-2618

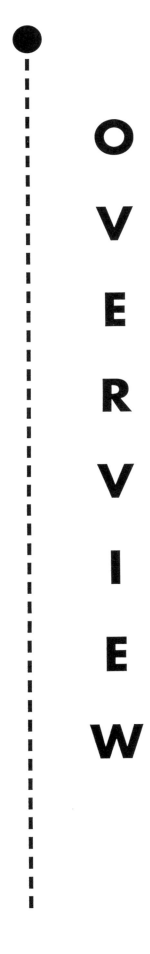

HISTORY & GEOGRAPHY

Curriculum Overview
Grades 1–12

	Grade 1	Grade 2	Grade 3
LIFEPAC 1	I AM A SPECIAL PERSON • God made me • You are God's child • All about you • Using proper manners	FAMILIES AND NEIGHBORS • We need a family • We help our family • Our neighborhood • Helping our neighbors	FISHING IN MAINE • A look at Deer Isle • A lobster boat • Planting lobster traps • Catching lobsters
LIFEPAC 2	COMMUNICATING WITH SOUND • Sounds people make • Sounds the communicate • Communicating without sound • Communicating with God	COMMUNITY HELPERS • What is a community • Community helpers • Your church community • Helping your community	FARMING IN KANSAS • The six parts of Kansas • Getting to know Kansas • Exploring Kansas • Harvest in Kansas
LIFEPAC 3	I HAVE FEELINGS • I feel sad • I feel afraid • A feel happy • I have other feelings	NEIGHBORHOOD STORES • Pioneer goods and services • Modern goods and services • Some business rules • God's business rules	FRUIT-GROWING IN WASHINGTON • Geography of Washington • Cities in Washington • Apple blossom time • Apple harvest time
LIFEPAC 4	I LIVE IN A FAMILY • My mother and father • My brothers and sisters • My grandparents • What my family does	FARMS AND CITIES • Farming long ago • Farming today • Growing cities • Changing cities	FORESTS IN OREGON • A land of forests • Trees of the forests • Lumbering in Oregon • Keeping Oregon's forests
LIFEPAC 5	YOU AND GOD'S FAMILY • Getting ready in the morning • Walking to school • The school family • The church family	NEIGHBORS AROUND THE WORLD • Things all families need • How communities share • How communities change • Customs of the world	CALIFORNIA: A GOLDEN LAND • Early California • The ranch community • A trip around the state • Work on a truck farm
LIFEPAC 6	PLACES PEOPLE LIVE • Life on the farm • Life in the city • Life by the sea	A JAPANESE FAMILY • Places people live in Japan • School in Japan • Work in Japan • Play in Japan	CATTLE IN TEXAS • Learning about Texas • Early ranches in Texas • Life on a ranch • A cattle round-up
LIFEPAC 7	COMMUNITY HELPERS • Firemen and policemen • Doctors • City workers • Teachers and ministers	HOW WE TRAVEL • Travel in Bible times • Travel in the past • Travel today • Changes in today's world	COAL MINING IN PENNSYLVANIA • The formation of coal • Products from coal • Methods of mining coal • The state of Pennsylvania
LIFEPAC 8	I LOVE MY COUNTRY • America discovered • The Pilgrims • The United States begin • Respect for your country	MESSAGES FROM FAR AND NEAR • Communication in Bible times • Communication today • Reasons for communication • Communication without sound	MANUFACTURING IN MICHIGAN • Facts about Michigan • Interesting people of Michigan • Places in Michigan • The treasures in Michigan
LIFEPAC 9	I LIVE IN THE WORLD • The globe • Countries • Friends in Mexico • Friends in Japan	CARING FOR OUR NEIGHBORHOODS • God's plan for nature • Sin changed nature • Problems in our neighborhoods • Helping our neighborhoods	SPACE TRAVEL IN FLORIDA • A place to launch spacecraft • Worker at the Space Center • The first flights • The trip to the moon
LIFEPAC 10	THE WORLD AND YOU • You are special • Your family • Your school and church • Your world	PEOPLE DEPEND ON EACH OTHER • Depending on our families • Depending on our neighbors • Depending on our communities • Communicating with God	REVIEW OF NINE STATES • California and Kansas • Washington and Maine • Oregon and Pennsylvania • Texas, Florida, and Michigan

Grade 4	Grade 5	Grade 6	
OUR EARTH • The surface of the earth • Early explorations of the earth • Exploring from space • Exploring the oceans	**A NEW WORLD** • Exploration of America • The first colonies • Conflict with Britain • Birth of the United States	**WORLD GEOGRAPHY** • Latitude and longitude • Western and eastern hemispheres • The southern hemisphere • Political and cultural regions	LIFEPAC 1
SEAPORT CITIES • Sydney • Hong Kong • Istanbul • London	**A NEW NATION** • War for Independence • Life in America • A new form of government • The Nation's early years	**THE CRADLE OF CIVILIZATION** • Mesopotamia • The land of Israel • The Nation of Israel • Egypt	LIFEPAC 2
DESERT LANDS • What is a desert? • Where are the deserts? • How do people live in the desert?	**A TIME OF TESTING** • Louisiana Purchase • War of 1812 • Sectionalism • Improvements in trade & travel	**GREECE AND ROME** • Geography of the region • Beginning civilizations • Contributions to other civilizations • The influence of Christianity	LIFEPAC 3
GRASSLANDS • Grasslands of the world • Ukraine • Kenya • Argentina	**A GROWING NATION** • Andrew Jackson's influence • Texas & Oregon • Mexican War • The Nation divides	**THE MIDDLE AGES** • The feudal system • Books and schools • The Crusades • Trade and architecture	LIFEPAC 4
TROPICAL RAIN FORESTS • Facts about rain forests • Rain forests of the world • The Amazon rain forest • The Congo rain forest	**A DIVIDED NATION** • Civil War • Reconstruction • Gilded Age • The need for reform	**SIX SOUTH AMERICAN COUNTRIES** • Brazil • Colombia • Venezuela • Three Guianas	LIFEPAC 5
THE POLAR REGIONS • The polar regions: coldest places in the world • The Arctic polar region • The Antarctic polar region	**A CHANGING NATION** • Progressive reforms • Spanish-American War • World War I • Roaring Twenties	**OTHER AMERICAN COUNTRIES** • Ecuador and Peru • Bolivia and Uruguay • Paraguay and Argentina • Chile	LIFEPAC 6
MOUNTAIN COUNTRIES • Peru – the Andes • The Incas and modern Peru • Nepal – the Himalayas • Switzerland – the Alps	**DEPRESSION AND WAR** • The Great Depression • War begins in Europe • War in Europe • War in the Pacific	**AFRICA** • Geography and cultures • Countries of northern Africa • Countries of central Africa • Countries of southern Africa	LIFEPAC 7
ISLAND COUNTRIES • Islands of the earth • Cuba • Iceland • Japan	**COLD WAR** • Korean War & other crises • Vietnam War • Civil Rights Movement • Upheaval in America	**MODERN WESTERN EUROPE** • The Renaissance • The Industrial Revolution • World War I • World War II	LIFEPAC 8
NORTH AMERICA • Geography • Lands, lakes and rivers • Northern countries • Southern countries	**THE END OF THE MILLENNIUM** • Watergate • Détente & Economic problems • The fall of Communism • Persian Gulf War	**MODERN EASTERN EUROPE** • Early government • Early churches • Early countries • Modern countries	LIFEPAC 9
OUR WORLD IN REVIEW • Europe and the explorers • Asia and Africa • Southern continents • North America, North Pole	**THE UNITED STATES OF AMERICA** • Review • Exploration & Founding • Expansion & Change • Superpower	**THE DEVELOPMENT OF OUR WORLD** • Cradle of civilization • The Middle Ages • Modern Europe • South America and Africa	LIFEPAC 10

History & Geography LIFEPAC Overview

	Grade 7	Grade 8	Grade 9
LIFEPAC 1	**WHAT IS HISTORY** • Definition and significance of history • Historians and the historical method • Views of history	**EUROPE COMES TO AMERICA** • Voyages of Columbus • Spanish exploration • Other exploration • The first colonies	**UNITED STATES HERITAGE** • American colonies • Acquisitions and annexations • Backgrounds to freedom • Backgrounds to society
LIFEPAC 2	**WHAT IS GEOGRAPHY** • Classes of geography • Geography and relief of the earth • Maps and the study of our world • Time zones	**BRITISH AMERICA** • English colonies • Government • Lifestyle • Wars with France	**OUR NATIONAL GOVERNMENT** • Ideals of national government • National government developed • Legislative and Executive branches • Judicial branch
LIFEPAC 3	**U.S. HISTORY AND GEOGRAPHY** • Geography of the U.S. • Early history of the U.S. • Physical regions of the U.S. • Cultural regions of the U.S.	**THE AMERICAN REVOLUTION** • British control • Rebellion of the Colonies • War for independence • Constitution	**STATE AND LOCAL GOVERNMENT** • Powers of state government • County government • Township government • City government
LIFEPAC 4	**ANTHROPOLOGY** • Understanding anthropology • The unity of man • The diversity of man • The culture of man	**A FIRM FOUNDATION** • Washington's presidency • Adams administration • Jeffersonian Democracy • War of 1812	**PLANNING A CAREER** • Definition of a career • God's will concerning a career • Selecting a career • Preparation for a career
LIFEPAC 5	**SOCIOLOGY** • Sociology defined • Historical development • Importance to Christians • Method of sociology	**A GROWING NATION** • Jacksonian Era • Northern border • Southern border • Industrial Revolution	**CITIZENSHIP** • Citizenship defined • Gaining citizenship • Rights of citizenship • Responsibilities of citizenship
LIFEPAC 6	**U.S. ANTHROPOLOGY** • Cultural background of the U.S. • Native American cultures • Cultures from distant lands • Cultural and social interaction	**THE CIVIL WAR** • Division & Session • Civil War • Death of Lincoln • Reconstruction	**THE EARTH AND MAN** • Man inhabits the earth • Man's home on the earth • Man develops the earth • The future of the earth
LIFEPAC 7	**ECONOMICS** • Economics defined • Methods of the economist • Tools of the economist • An experiment in economy	**GILDED AGE TO PROGRESSIVE ERA** • Rise of industry • Wild West • America as a world power • Progressive era	**REGIONS OF THE WORLD** • A region defined • Geographic and climate regions • Cultural and political regions • Economic regions of Europe
LIFEPAC 8	**POLITICAL SCIENCE** • Definition of political science • Roots of Western thought • Modern political thinkers • Political theory	**A WORLD IN CONFLICT** • World War I • Great Depression • New Deal • World War II	**MAN AND HIS ENVIRONMENT** • The physical environment • Drug abuse • The social environment • Man's responsibilities
LIFEPAC 9	**STATE ECONOMICS AND POLITICS** • Background of state government • State government • State finance • State politics	**COLD WAR AMERICA** • Origins of the Cold War • Vietnam • Truman to Nixon • Ending of the Cold War	**TOOLS OF THE GEOGRAPHER** • The globe • Types of maps • Reading maps • The earth in symbol form
LIFEPAC 10	**SOCIAL SCIENCES REVIEW** • History and geography • Anthropology • Sociology • Economics and politics	**RECENT AMERICA & REVIEW** • Europe to independence • Colonies to the Civil War • Civil War to World War II • World War II through Cold War	**MAN IN A CHANGING WORLD** • Development of the nation • Development of government • Development of the earth • Solving problems

Grade 10	Grade 11	Grade 12	
ANCIENT CIVILIZATION • Origin of civilization • Early Egypt • Assyria and Babylonia • Persian civilization	FOUNDATIONS OF DEMOCRACY • Democracy develops • Virginia • New England colonies • Middle and southern colonies	INTERNATIONAL GOVERNMENTS • Why have governments • Types of governments • Governments in our world • Political thinkers	LIFEPAC 1
ANCIENT CIVILIZATIONS • India • China • Greek civilization • Roman Empire	CONSTITUTIONAL GOVERNMENT • Relations with England • The Revolutionary War • Articles of Confederation • Constitution of the U.S.	UNITED STATES GOVERNMENT • U.S. Constitution • Bill of Rights • Three branches of government • Legislative process	LIFEPAC 2
THE MEDIEVAL WORLD • Introduction to Middle Ages • Early Middle Ages • Middle Ages in transition • High Middle Ages	NATIONAL EXPANSION • A strong federal government • Revolution of 1800 • War of 1812 • Nationalism and sectionalism	AMERICAN PARTY SYSTEM • American party system • Development political parties • Functions of political parties • Voting	LIFEPAC 3
RENAISSANCE AND REFORMATION • Changes in government and art • Changes in literature and thought • Advances in science • Reform within the Church	A NATION DIVIDED • Issues of division • Division of land and people • Economics of slavery • Politics of slavery	HISTORY OF GOVERNMENTS • Primitive governments • Beginnings of Democracy • Feudalism, Theocracy & Democracy • Fascism & Nazism	LIFEPAC 4
GROWTH OF WORLD EMPIRES • England and France • Portugal and Spain • Austria and Germany • Italy and the Ottoman Empire	A NATION UNITED AGAIN • Regionalism • The division • The Civil War • Reconstruction	THE CHRISTIAN & GOVERNMENT • Discrimination & the Christian • Christian attitudes • "Opinion & Truth" in politics • Politics & Propaganda	LIFEPAC 5
THE AGE OF REVOLUTION • Factors leading to revolution • The English Revolution • The American Revolution • The French Revolution	INVOLVEMENT AT HOME & ABROAD • Surge of industry • The industrial lifestyle • Isolationism • Involvement in conflict	FREE ENTERPRISE • Economics • Competition • Money through history • International finance & currency	LIFEPAC 6
THE INDUSTRIAL REVOLUTION • Sparks of preparation • Industrial revolution in England • Industrial revolution in America • Social changes of the revolution	THE SEARCH FOR PEACE • The War and its aftermath • The Golden Twenties • The Great Depression • The New Deal	BUSINESS AND YOU • Running a business • Government & business • Banks & Mergers • Deregulation & Bankruptcy	LIFEPAC 7
TWO WORLD WARS • Mounting tension • World War I • Peace and power quests • World War II	A NATION AT WAR • Causes of the war • World War II • Korean Conflict • Vietnam Conflict	THE STOCK MARKET • How it started and works • Selecting stocks • Types of stocks • Tracking stocks	LIFEPAC 8
THE CONTEMPORARY WORLD • Korean War • International organizations • Atomic stalemate • A form of coexistence	CONTEMPORARY AMERICA • Kennedy's New Frontier • Johnson's Great Society • Nixon's New Internationalism • Ford and a new era	BUDGET AND FINANCE • Cash, Credit & Checking • Buying a car • Grants, Loans & IRAs • Savings & E-cash	LIFEPAC 9
ANCIENT TIMES TO THE PRESENT • Ancient civilizations • Medieval times • The Renaissance • The modern world	UNITED STATES HISTORY • Basis of democracy • The 1800's • Industrialization • Current history	GEOGRAPHY AND REVIEW • Euro & International finance • U.S. Geography • The global traveler • Neighbors, Heroes & The Holy Land	LIFEPAC 10

MANAGEMENT

STRUCTURE OF THE LIFEPAC CURRICULUM

The LIFEPAC curriculum is conveniently structured to provide one teacher handbook containing teacher support material with answer keys and ten student worktexts for each subject at grade levels two through twelve. The worktext format of the LIFEPACs allows the student to read the textual information and complete workbook activities all in the same booklet. The easy to follow LIFEPAC numbering system lists the grade as the first number(s) and the last two digits as the number of the series. For example, the Language Arts LIFEPAC at the 6th grade level, 5th book in the series would be LA 605.

Each LIFEPAC is divided into 3 to 5 sections and begins with an introduction or overview of the booklet as well as a series of specific learning objectives to give a purpose to the study of the LIFEPAC. The introduction and objectives are followed by a vocabulary section which may be found at the beginning of each section at the lower levels, at the beginning of the LIFEPAC in the middle grades, or in the glossary at the high school level. Vocabulary words are used to develop word recognition and should not be confused with the spelling words introduced later in the LIFEPAC. The student should learn all vocabulary words before working the LIFEPAC sections to improve comprehension, retention, and reading skills.

Each activity or written assignment has a number for easy identification, such as 1.1. The first number corresponds to the LIFEPAC section and the number to the right of the decimal is the number of the activity.

Teacher checkpoints, which are essential to maintain quality learning, are found at various locations throughout the LIFEPAC. The teacher should check 1) neatness of work and penmanship, 2) quality of understanding (tested with a short oral quiz), 3) thoroughness of answers (complete sentences and paragraphs, correct spelling, etc.), 4) completion of activities (no blank spaces), and 5) accuracy of answers as compared to the answer key (all answers correct).

The self test questions are also number coded for easy reference. For example, 2.015 means that this is the 15th question in the self test of Section II. The first number corresponds to the LIFEPAC section, the zero indicates that it is a self test question, and the number to the right of the zero the question number.

The LIFEPAC test is packaged at the centerfold of each LIFEPAC. It should be removed and put aside before giving the booklet to the student for study.

Answer and test keys have the same numbering system as the LIFEPACs and appear at the back of this handbook. The student may be given access to the answer keys (not the test keys) under teacher supervision so that he can score his own work.

A thorough study of the Curriculum Overview by the teacher before instruction begins is essential to the success of the student. The teacher should become familiar with expected skill mastery and understand how these grade level skills fit into the overall skill development of the curriculum. The teacher should also preview the objectives that appear at the beginning of each LIFEPAC for additional preparation and planning.

TEST SCORING and GRADING

Answer keys and test keys give examples of correct answers. They convey the idea, but the student may use many ways to express a correct answer. The teacher should check for the essence of the answer, not for the exact wording. Many questions are high level and require thinking and creativity on the part of the student. Each answer should be scored based on whether or not the main idea written by the student matches the model example. "Any Order" or "Either Order" in a key indicates that no particular order is necessary to be correct.

Most self tests and LIFEPAC tests at the lower elementary levels are scored at 1 point per answer; however, the upper levels may have a point system awarding 2 to 5 points for various answers or questions. Further, the total test points will vary; they may not always equal 100 points. They may be 78, 85, 100, 105, etc.

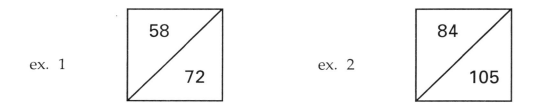

A score box similar to ex.1 above is located at the end of each self test and on the front of the LIFEPAC test. The bottom score, 72, represents the total number of points possible on the test. The upper score, 58, represents the number of points your student will need to receive an 80% or passing grade. If you wish to establish the exact percentage that your student has achieved, find the total points of his correct answers and divide it by the bottom number (in this case 72.) For example, if your student has a point total of 65, divide 65 by 72 for a grade of 90%. Referring to ex. 2, on a test with a total of 105 possible points, the student would have to receive a minimum of 84 correct points for an 80% or passing grade. If your student has received 93 points, simply divide the 93 by 105 for a percentage grade of 86%. Students who receive a score below 80% should review the LIFEPAC and retest using the appropriate Alternate Test found in the Teacher's Guide.

The following is a guideline to assign letter grades for completed LIFEPACs based on a maximum total score of 100 points.

LIFEPAC Test   =   60% of the Total Score (or percent grade)
Self Test   =   25% of the Total Score (average percent of self tests)
Reports   =   10% or 10* points per LIFEPAC
Oral Work   =   5% or 5* points per LIFEPAC
*Determined by the teacher's subjective evaluation of the student's daily work.

Example:

LIFEPAC Test Score	=	92%	92	x	.60	=	55 points
Self Test Average	=	90%	90	x	.25	=	23 points
Reports						=	8 points
Oral Work						=	4 points

TOTAL POINTS   =   90 points

Grade Scale based on point system:

100	–	94	=	A
93	–	86	=	B
85	–	77	=	C
76	–	70	=	D
Below		70	=	F

TEACHER HINTS and STUDYING TECHNIQUES

LIFEPAC Activities are written to check the level of understanding of the preceding text. The student may look back to the text as necessary to complete these activities; however, a student should never attempt to do the activities without reading (studying) the text first. Self tests and LIFEPAC tests are never open book tests.

Language arts activities (skill integration) often appear within other subject curriculum. The purpose is to give the student an opportunity to test his skill mastery outside of the context in which it was presented.

Writing complete answers (paragraphs) to some questions is an integral part of the LIFEPAC Curriculum in all subjects. This builds communication and organization skills, increases understanding and retention of ideas, and helps enforce good penmanship. Complete sentences should be encouraged for this type of activity. Obviously, single words or phrases do not meet the intent of the activity, since multiple lines are given for the response.

Review is essential to student success. Time invested in review where review is suggested will be time saved in correcting errors later. Self tests, unlike the section activities, are closed book. This procedure helps to identify weaknesses before they become too great to overcome. Certain objectives from self tests are cumulative and test previous sections; therefore, good preparation for a self test must include all material studied up to that testing point.

The following procedure checklist has been found to be successful in developing good study habits in the LIFEPAC curriculum.

1. Read the introduction and Table of Contents.
2. Read the objectives.
3. Recite and study the entire vocabulary (glossary) list.
4. Study each section as follows:
    a. Read the introduction and study the section objectives.
    b. Read all the text for the entire section, but answer none of the activities.
    c. Return to the beginning of the section and memorize each vocabulary word and definition.
    d. Reread the section, complete the activities, check the answers with the answer key, correct all errors, and have the teacher check.
    e. Read the self test but do not answer the questions.
    f. Go to the beginning of the first section and reread the text and answers to the activities up to the self test you have not yet done.
    g. Answer the questions to the self test without looking back.
    h. Have the self test checked by the teacher.
    i. Correct the self test and have the teacher check the corrections.
    j. Repeat steps a–i for each section.

5. Use the SQ3R* method to prepare for the LIFEPAC test.
6. Take the LIFEPAC test as a closed book test.
7. LIFEPAC tests are administered and scored under direct teacher supervision. Students who receive scores below 80% should review the LIFEPAC using the SQ3R* study method and take the Alternate Test located in the Teacher Handbook. The final test grade may be the grade on the Alternate Test or an average of the grades from the original LIFEPAC test and the Alternate Test.

    *SQ3R: Scan the whole LIFEPAC.

        Question yourself on the objectives.

        Read the whole LIFEPAC again.

        Recite through an oral examination.

        Review weak areas.

GOAL SETTING and SCHEDULES

Each school must develop its own schedule, because no single set of procedures will fit every situation. The following is an example of a daily schedule that includes the five LIFEPAC subjects as well as time slotted for special activities.

Possible Daily Schedule

8:15	–	8:25	Pledges, prayer, songs, devotions, etc.
8:25	–	9:10	Bible
9:10	–	9:55	Language Arts
9:55	–	10:15	Recess (juice break)
10:15	–	11:00	Mathematics
11:00	–	11:45	History & Geography
11:45	–	12:30	Lunch, recess, quiet time
12:30	–	1:15	Science
1:15	–		Drill, remedial work, enrichment*

*Enrichment: Computer time, physical education, field trips, fun reading, games and puzzles, family business, hobbies, resource persons, guests, crafts, creative work, electives, music appreciation, projects.

Basically, two factors need to be considered when assigning work to a student in the LIFEPAC curriculum.

The first is time. An average of 45 minutes should be devoted to each subject, each day. Remember, this is only an average. Because of extenuating circumstances a student may spend only 15 minutes on a subject one day and the next day spend 90 minutes on the same subject.

The second factor is the number of pages to be worked in each subject. A single LIFEPAC is designed to take 3 to 4 weeks to complete. Allowing about 3-4 days for LIFEPAC introduction, review, and tests, the student has approximately 15 days to complete the LIFEPAC pages. Simply take the number of pages in the LIFEPAC, divide it by 15 and you will have the number of pages that must be completed on a daily basis to keep the student on schedule. For example, a LIFEPAC containing 45 pages will require 3 completed pages per day. Again, this is only an average. While working a 45 page LIFEPAC, the student may complete only 1 page the first day if the text has a lot of activities or reports, but go on to complete 5 pages the next day.

Long range planning requires some organization. Because the traditional school year originates in the early fall of one year and continues to late spring of the following year, a calendar should be devised that covers this period of time. Approximate beginning and completion dates can be noted on the calendar as well as special occasions such as holidays, vacations and birthdays. Since each LIFEPAC takes 3-4 weeks or eighteen days to complete, it should take about 180 school days to finish a set of ten LIFEPACs. Starting at the beginning school date, mark off eighteen school days on the calendar and that will become the targeted completion date for the first LIFEPAC. Continue marking the calendar until you have established dates for the remaining nine LIFEPACs making adjustments for previously noted holidays and vacations. If all five subjects are being used, the ten established target dates should be the same for the LIFEPACs in each subject.

FORMS

The sample weekly lesson plan and student grading sheet forms are included in this section as teacher support materials and may be duplicated at the convenience of the teacher.

The student grading sheet is provided for those who desire to follow the suggested guidelines for assignment of letter grades found on page 3 of this section. The student's self test scores should be posted as percentage grades. When the LIFEPAC is completed the teacher should average the self test grades, multiply the average by .25 and post the points in the box marked self test points. The LIFEPAC percentage grade should be multiplied by .60 and posted. Next, the teacher should award and post points for written reports and oral work. A report may be any type of written work assigned to the student whether it is a LIFEPAC or additional learning activity. Oral work includes the student's ability to respond orally to questions which may or may not be related to LIFEPAC activities or any type of oral report assigned by the teacher. The points may then be totaled and a final grade entered along with the date that the LIFEPAC was completed.

The Student Record Book which was specifically designed for use with the Alpha Omega curriculum provides space to record weekly progress for one student over a nine week period as well as a place to post self test and LIFEPAC scores. The Student Record Books are available through the current Alpha Omega catalog; however, unlike the enclosed forms these books are not for duplication and should be purchased in sets of four to cover a full academic year.

WEEKLY LESSON PLANNER

Week of:

	Subject	Subject	Subject	Subject
Monday				
Tuesday				
Wednesday				
Thursday				
Friday				

WEEKLY LESSON PLANNER

Week of:

	Subject	Subject	Subject	Subject
Monday				
	Subject	Subject	Subject	Subject
Tuesday				
	Subject	Subject	Subject	Subject
Wednesday				
	Subject	Subject	Subject	Subject
Thursday				
	Subject	Subject	Subject	Subject
Friday				

Student Name _____   Year _____

Bible

LP #	Self Test Scores by Sections 1	2	3	4	5	Self Test Points	LIFEPAC Test	Oral Points	Report Points	Final Grade	Date
01											
02											
03											
04											
05											
06											
07											
08											
09											
10											

History & Geography

LP #	Self Test Scores by Sections 1	2	3	4	5	Self Test Points	LIFEPAC Test	Oral Points	Report Points	Final Grade	Date
01											
02											
03											
04											
05											
06											
07											
08											
09											
10											

Language Arts

LP #	Self Test Scores by Sections 1	2	3	4	5	Self Test Points	LIFEPAC Test	Oral Points	Report Points	Final Grade	Date
01											
02											
03											
04											
05											
06											
07											
08											
09											
10											

Student Name _____   Year _____

Mathematics

LP #	Self Test Scores by Sections 1	2	3	4	5	Self Test Points.	LIFEPAC Test	Oral Points	Report Points	Final Grade	Date
01											
02											
03											
04											
05											
06											
07											
08											
09											
10											

Science

LP #	Self Test Scores by Sections 1	2	3	4	5	Self Test Points	LIFEPAC Test	Oral Points	Report Points	Final Grade	Date
01											
02											
03											
04											
05											
06											
07											
08											
09											
10											

Spelling/Electives

LP #	Self Test Scores by Sections 1	2	3	4	5	Self Test Points	LIFEPAC Test	Oral Points	Report Points	Final Grade	Date
01											
02											
03											
04											
05											
06											
07											
08											
09											
10											

NOTES

INSTRUCTIONS FOR HISTORY & GEOGRAPHY

The LIFEPAC curriculum from grades two through twelve is structured so that the daily instructional material is written directly into the LIFEPACs. The student is encouraged to read and follow this instructional material in order to develop independent study habits. The teacher should introduce the LIFEPAC to the student, set a required completion schedule, complete teacher checks, be available for questions regarding both content and procedures, administer and grade tests, and develop additional learning activities as desired. Teachers working with several students may schedule their time so that students are assigned to a quiet work activity when it is necessary to spend instructional time with one particular student.

The Teacher Notes section of the Teacher's Guide lists the required or suggested materials for the LIFEPACs and provides additional learning activities for the students. The materials section refers only to LIFEPAC materials and does not include materials which may be needed for the additional activities. Additional learning activities provide a change from the daily school routine, encourage the student's interest in learning and may be used as a reward for good study habits.

MATERIALS NEEDED for LIFEPAC:

Required:

Suggested:
pictures of different kinds of boats
pictures of lobsters and other crustaceans
banner paper, toothpicks
white glue
clay, scissors, paste, drawing paper,
construction paper, writing paper
oatmeal boxes
old socks
light cardboard (may be found in shirt
packages, hose packages)
water colors
salt clay: boil 3 cups salt in 1 1/2 cups
water. Add small amount of cold water to
1 1/2 cups cornstarch. Add to salt and stir
briskly until thick. Wrap tightly in foil
paper.

ADDITIONAL LEARNING ACTIVITIES

Section I *Discovering Deer Isle*

1. Discuss these questions with your class.
   a. Why did Kim and Mark have to cross a bridge to get to Uncle Jack's?
   b. Can you name the states through which they had to travel?
   c. Why was the bridge high in the middle?
   d. How big is Deer Ie?
   e. Why do you suppose they have what is called a "General Store" on Deer Isle?
   f. Why did Uncle Jack like the "fishy" smell?
   g. What were some of the things they saw from the boat on that first day's ride?
2. Display pictures of many kinds of boats. Identify those that would be used by fisherman. Discuss reasons why.
3. Assign students to committees. Make a large "walk on" map (on banner paper) of Deer Isle—buildings, quarry, and so forth (maybe some boats to put in the bay). Students may use the map to "travel" the route Kim and Mark followed to get to Uncle Jack's and also the route of the first boat ride.
4. Ask students to write a short description of the inside of the General Store. (Include food, traps, furniture, clothing, and articles for boats.)
5. Students may use clay to "build" a fisherman's boat.
6. Have students write a short "story" describing one of the small towns on the way to Uncle Jack's place. If desired and time permits, the story may be illustrated.
7. Have students draw a picture of Uncle Jack's community. It may be panorama style or map style. If the teacher so desires, the pictures may be shared with the class or displayed on the bulletin board.

Section II *Planting Lobster Traps*

1. Discuss these questions with your class.
   a. Why can't lobster traps be set and left?
   b. What does a lobster trap look like?
   c. How does a lobster get into the trap?
   d. What is another name for a lobster trap?
   e. What else must you have to set a lobster trap?
   f. How do the lobsters warn each other about how close they are?
   g. Why are lobster pots so heavy?
   h. How do the men "set the lobster traps" and get lobsters?
   i. Why do they put small lobsters back into the sea?
   j. What did Mark and Kim learn at the quarry?
   k. What were the auction, the gallery, and the museum like?
   l. Are herrings the same thing as sardines?
2. Make a lobster pot. Cut strips of brown construction paper to paste as slats on the sides of an oatmeal box. Glue the top of an old sock, that has been cut above the heel part, to the end of the box so that the top of the old sock will fit inside the oatmeal box to represent the "net" trap that the lobster walks into.
3. Display pictures of crustaceans. Discuss lobster fishing. (Why do we have people who do lobster fishing as their work?)
4. Write two or three sentences telling how Uncle Jack "set" his lobster traps.
5. Have students write and illustrate a story about the quarry.
6. Allow students to use watercolors to make a picture they might "hang" in an art gallery.
7. Have students write and share with the class a story about a day they would like to spend on an island like Deer Isle.

Section III *Catching Lobsters*

1. Discuss these questions with your class.
   a. How do the lobster fishermen know where their pots are?
   b. How do they keep the lobsters from harming each other?
   c. Where do they put the lobsters after they take them from the pots?
   d. What happens to lobster shells when they are outgrown?
2. Have students write a report describing a lobster. It may be with illustrations. Find more information in the encyclopedia.
3. Draw a large picture of a lobster. Label all the parts at the side and make arrows to show the location of each part.
4. Have students pretend they are lobsters. Have them write how they happened to get into a lobster trap and what they planned to do next.
5. Have students write a short essay on how a lobster looks for food and what kinds of things he might eat. Illustrate the writing.
6. Have students make a lobster from salt clay (see Materials Needed). When the clay has completely dried (usually one to two days), paint it the color of a lobster.

MATERIALS NEEDED for LIFEPAC:

Required:
map of United States
drawing paper
writing paper
crayons
chalk

Suggested:
bird seed
large container like a sandbox
picture of wheat fields, combines, and
other farm machinery
blue construction paper
yellow and brown crepe paper
tagboard and cardboard (from boxes and
from hosiery packages)
small stones
toothpicks
small boxes, various sizes and shapes
oatmeal box or cylindrical can
paints, string, clay, and hair spray or
chalk fixative

ADDITIONAL LEARNING ACTIVITIES

Section I *Flying into Kansas*

1. Discuss these questions with your class.
   a. Why do you suppose the plane landed in Topeka instead of Lebanon?
   b. Why did Grandmother not come to meet Judie and Paul?
   c. Why was Grandfather concerned about the clouds?
   d. What is a "soaker" rain?
   e. What did the land near the farm look like?
   f. What is a dugout?
   g. How many parts did Grandfather draw on his map of Kansas? Can you name them?
   h. Can you tell what you might find in each section?
2. Plant grass seed (rye) thickly in a flat, long container. It should come up quickly and resemble a "wheat field." When the seed begins to get high, students may cut it as a farmer does (top part). If a large sandbox (for example) is used, students might divide the container into "fields."
3. Show a map of Kansas. Ask students to identify each part (as in LIFEPAC).
4. Students may show on a United States map where they live and how they might fly to Topeka, Kansas.
5. Have each student research how wheat becomes flour. Write a paper explaining the process.
6. Draw a large 12 x 18 picture of Grandfather's farm.

Section II *Getting to Know Kansas*

1. Discuss these questions with your class.
   a. What is a dugout?
   b. What are soddies?
   c. What is the difference between a dugout and a soddy?
   d. What is the geographical center of the United States?
   e. How did Judie and Paul know where the geographical center of the

31

United States was?
   f. Why is Kansas called the Breadbasket of the Nation?
   g. What happened to make Kansas become known as a dust bowl?
   h. What is the state flower of Kansas?
2. Have students discuss "one day of living in a dugout" or "one day of living in a soddie."
3. Make a sunflower. Cut a circle the size of a paper plate from tagboard. Draw a smaller circle in the middle of the circle. Cut petal shapes from yellow crepe paper. Stretch the wide end to make it cup up. Paste these petals on the outer circle with the wide end, where it has been stretched, being the end that is pasted. Keep making rows of these petals until the outer circle has been covered. Cut brown crepe paper into 1" squares. Press each square around the eraser end of the pencil, dip in paste, and press into the center circle (makes the "face" of the sunflower). A stem may be cut from tagboard, if teacher so desires, and colored green.

Section III   *Exploring Kansas*
1. Discuss these questions with your class.
   a. Why is Dr. Brewster Higley famous?
   b. What are petroglyphs?
   c. Who are some of the western people honored in Kansas?
   d. Why were shark teeth found in Kansas?
   e. What is a game preserve?
   f. Why is Dodge City called the Cowboy Capital of the World?
   g. How do we get the salt we eat?
   h. What is strip mining? What are people doing to correct the damage done by strip mining?
   i. What was the Bible Parade like?
   j. What are some "kinds" of Bibles the children saw in the Bible collection?
   k. Why is Abilene an important Kansas town?
   l. What are stone fence posts?
   m. Why did settlers not use trees for buildings and fences?
2. Learn and sing the words to "Home on the Range."
3. On pieces of cardboard (9" x 12") have committees design and make a float for the Bible Parade. (Use stand up figures, clay figures, dolls, etc. Students may bring articles from home for this project.) Then have a Bible Parade— maybe for another classroom.
4. As a group let students share the "petroglyph" stories they wrote on page 31 in their LIFEPAC.

Independent Activities
5. On blue construction paper, have students draw pictures of the Pioneer Section (LIFEPAC, page 32) with white chalk. Spray with hair spray or fixative.
6. Have students research the silo and write about how it functions. Then make a silo from an oatmeal box or any cylindrical box or can.
7. Judie and Paul visited many interesting places in Kansas. Pick one place they visited. Pretend that you and your friends meet Judie and Paul at that spot. Write about meeting them. What do they tell you about their trip? What can

you tell them about places you have been or read about in books? Use good sentences. Use good cursive writing. Write this report on LIFEPAC Tablet 300. Teacher will check to see if student has utilized knowledge gained from the LIFEPAC.

Section IV *Harvesting in Kansas*

1. Discuss these questions with your class.
    a. Why are farmers afraid of rain at harvest time?
    b. How are the trucks loaded?
    c. Where does the wheat go after it leaves the fields?
    d. After the wheat is harvested, what happens to the fields?
    e. How do a disk and a harrow work?

2. Display pictures of wheat fields. Discuss how wheat is grown and harvested. Talk about some of the difficulties in raising wheat.

3. Give students the opportunity to research the growing and harvesting of wheat. Have them make reports on some aspects of it.

4. Have students write short stories from the worker's point of view telling how wheat is harvested. Student could pretend he is the combine driver.

5. Have students make a close-up picture of a combine. (They may need to use an encyclopedia or other reference books.)

MATERIALS NEEDED for LIFEPAC:

Suggested:
United States map
book on travel in Washington
picture book on apple growing

ADDITIONAL LEARNING ACTIVITIES
Section I *A New Home in Washington*
1. Discuss these questions with your class.
    a. Have you ever met anyone from Washington? How far is Washington from us here in____? How would you get to Washington? What are some of the states you would pass through if you drove to Washington?
    b. Do you suppose there are many Canadians living in Washington? Why?
    c. Washington is next to the Pacific Ocean: how much of the year would it be possible to swim in the ocean? Do you know anyone from Oregon or Idaho? How similar would life in those two states (Oregon and Idaho) be to life in Washington?
    d. Washington has a beautiful river (Columbia), a huge dam, and majestic mountains. Which of these would you like to live close to? What big city would you be closest to?
2. Let each student draw and then cut out a scale model of one of the following states: Idaho, Washington, Oregon, or Western Canada. (Let one inch = 300 miles. Parents, of course, will have to assist in the drawing phase to keep the cut-outs to a uniform scale.) Let the students then bring the cutouts to class for purposes of making a jigsaw map of the Pacific Northwest.
3. Have a drawing contest (using blackboard or plain paper) to see which student can come closest to the shape of the state of Washington.
4. Let students represent the four areas in this section: Southwest Canada, Idaho, Oregon, and Washington. Standing in proper relationship to one another, let the students tell something of the climate and geography of the area they represent. Then let the students join in a circle and declare themselves the total perimeter of the Northwest Territory. At this point let each student make his original statement, this time declaring, "The Northwest is _____."
5. Let the students discuss where they would like to go in Washington for a camping trip (i.e., the Columbia River area, Grand Coulee Dam, or the Cascade Mountains). Students should tell about the many attractions of the area they visit. Then let the class vote on the area that seems to offer the most enjoyment for camping.
6. Have an elimination contest: on a blank map of Washington let students take turns drawing in the mountains, rivers, cities, and so forth, one item per turn. When a student can no longer add something accurately to the map, he is eliminated.
7. A student draws a map of the state of Washington paying special attention to the bordering regions. Let the student draw something that characterizes the neighboring area (e.g., fish leaping out of the water for the Pacific, a potato for Idaho, etc.).

8. Let the student find some information about Washington's Pacific coastline. Let the student write about the climate there throughout the seasons.

9. Let the student look for information on the Grand Coulee Dam. When was it built? How long did it take to build it? How much did it cost? What changes did it bring to Washington?

10. Let the student find information on the Columbia River. When is the finest fishing season? Where are the favorite campsites? How much of the river is in Canada?

11. Let the student research the population figures of Washington's major cities. Let the student seek to determine why so many people chose that city above other cities to live (i.e., to what extent did geography play a part in the growth and development of the large city the student chooses?).

12. Write about recreation in Washington during the four seasons; the various problems children encounter on the west side of the Cascades because of the excessive rainfall could be presented. Write about why people move to Washington and how life is different in Washington compared to life where the student lives. Guide the student in making comparisons, proving ideas, and drawing conclusions.

Section II *Apple Blossom Time*

1. Discuss these questions with your class.
   a. Do you think an apple grower has much free time in the winter? What would happen if he did his pruning and grafting in the summer? What might happen to an apple orchard if a farmer skipped three winters of pruning his trees?
   b. Do you think spring is a busier time for apple growers than winter? What essential work is done in the spring?
   c. Do bees do work for the apple grower that man would have to do if there were no bees in the area? How do bees carry pollen from one tree to another?
   d. What job do you think you would prefer in an apple orchard? What do you think the easiest job would be? The hardest?
   e. Can you name three critical points in apple growing (i.e., jobs which, if neglected, or done away with, or done improperly, would ruin the harvest?)
   f. Could you properly graft a branch onto an apple tree if you had your father help you (i.e., could you tell him how to do it)?

2. Set up a mock apple orchard of twelve trees, using thin slats or old brooms driven into the ground. Be careful to properly space the trees. Let the students take turns acting as foreman, describing the job process he would follow to bring in a rich harvest.

3. Let various students assume the roles of workers in the orchard (i.e., pickers, sorters, pruners, packers, and blossom trimmers). Let each student, in proper sequence, describe the essential purpose of his process and the key to doing it properly.

4. Make a group poster, drawing the major phases of apple growing in simple, symbolic sketches.

5. Arrange to visit a bee farm. Visit with the purpose of learning about the bees' nectar gathering activity and how the by-product (pollination) assists in the growth process of the plants the bees visit.
6. Let a student write a report on grafting: the purpose and its results.
7. Let a student plan an imaginary orchard. How many trees will he plant? How long will he have to wait for them to bear fruit (from the time they are planted as saplings)? How many workers will he need? What kind of a processing plant will he build and what kind of equipment will he want in the building? How will he find workers for harvest time?
8. Let a student do a book report on beekeeping.
9. Let a student picture (in three sketches) a bee: (a) sucking the nectar while gathering pollen on its feet, (b) flying to another blossom, and (c) depositing the pollen on another blossom.

Section III   *Apple Harvest Time*
1. Discuss these questions with your class.
   a. Do you know what kind of apples your mother buys most often for the family? What is your preference?
   b. Do you think one type of apple would be any more difficult to grow than any other?
   c. Will you have more appreciation for an apple the next time you hold it in your hand? How many processes (jobs) go into bringing an apple to the fruit shelf of your local grocery?
   d. If you were an apple grower, would you prefer machines or people for the harvesting?
2. Let someone obtain a book on apple growing from the library. The book should have large pictures. Let the student, with the book held open at various pages containing pictures depicting the processes of apple growing, have students volunteer to name and describe the process pictured in the book.
3. Let each student select a kind of apple and then call on a local grocer (at a time when he would not be too busy) to ask what time of the year that particular apple is in season, cheapest, and most expensive?
4. Ask a grocer if your group may go back into the cold storage to see how the apples are packaged and stored.
5. Using pictures from a book on apple growing, let a student draw each of the four apples pictured on page 43, being careful to color each properly.
6. Let a student write a letter to a chamber of commerce in the state of Washington (Olympia, Washington) asking for a brochure on one of the Apple Growers Festivals in that state.
7. Let a student purchase three or four different kinds of apples. Cut them down the middle (top to bottom) and analyze the differences in the core of each apple.

MATERIALS NEEDED for LIFEPAC:

Suggested:
a picture book on lumbering from the library
World Book: the section on Oregon, Lumbering

ADDITIONAL LEARNING ACTIVITIES

Section I *Looking at Oregon*

1. Discuss these questions with your class.
    a. Have you ever been to Oregon? How would you get there from here by car? What are some of the states you would drive through?
    b. Do you know of any islands that were formed by volcanoes? (The point of this question is that Oregon was formed in large part by volcanoes.)
    c. Would deep sea divers be able to discover where the water in Crater Lake comes from, goes to?
    d. Do you know where the big forests are in our state?
    e. Do you think only big strong men can do the work of a lumberman? (Answer: No. The climbers and river rats tend to be small and light on their feet.)
2. Take a trip to a nearby woods. Look for (a) wolf trees, (b) diseased trees, (c) trees that may be over 100 years old, and (d) the presence of birds in the woods (protecting the trees by removing insects).
3. Let each student assume the role of a bordering territory (of Oregon). Take positions at the center point of each border line. Let the student, as his turn comes, verbalize, with arms spread to either side, "I am (name of his state or territory) and my borders with Oregon run _____ miles on either side of me."
4. Let a student write an Oregon chamber of commerce for a "travel in Oregon" brochure.
5. Let a student do a study (using World Book or Compton's) on Oregon's forests. Aim to determine (a) how many people in Oregon work in the industry, (b) how many major cities were built around the lumber industry, and (c) what major fires there have been in the last twenty years.
6. Let a student draw a map of Oregon coloring in (a) areas of dense forest, (b) major cities, and (c) major bodies of water.

Section II *Lumbering in Oregon*

1. Discuss these questions with your class.
    a. If you lived in Oregon which of the lumberman's jobs would you most like to have?
    b. Some lumbermen have to have strong arms, others have to be light on their feet. What would happen if the river rats had to do the chopping and the cat skinners had to pull the logs to the trucks?
    c. Does it seem to you that there is one job in the logging show that is more important than any other?
2. List each of the jobs of a "logging show" on slips of paper. Let students draw the pieces of paper from a hat. The following day let each student (in order that

the job is done in the logging show) describe his job from the point where the previous job leaves off and the next begins.

3. Let students take turns in acting as a foreman who is in the process of hiring workers for a "logging show." The foreman should explain what he is looking for in each specific worker. Let the teacher judge which foreman has the most understanding of the "logging show."

4. Let a student do a book report on a story about a lumberjack camp.

5. Let a student describe in drawings the process of a logging show.

6. Let a student visit a local lumberyard to learn which of the cords of lumber in stock has come from Oregon. Ask questions about the features of the various types of (Oregon) lumber. Make a report on this visit.

Section III   *Keeping Oregon's Forests*

1. Discuss these questions with your class.
   a. Why do you suppose lumbermen drop many more seeds on the ground than the number of trees they want? (Answer: The birds eat many of the seeds; others fall on rock, etc.)
   b. Is it enough to just let the seedlings grow wild and wait until they have grown to full size before sending workers in among them? (Answer: No. A thinning process must be carried out in the growing stage.)
   c. Would you like to be a smoke jumper? How dangerous do you think the job is?
   d. Have you heard about any big forest fires in the last year? What is the best way to fight a fire? (Answer: Get to it before it gets too big.)
   e. Does it cost your family when there is a series of big forest fires? (Answer: Yes, it makes the cost of lumber higher; houses become more expensive, etc.)

2. Act out a skit where a fire spotter calls the foreman of a firefighter crew. The foreman then asks (a) how long has the fire been going? (b) How big is the fire now? (c) How much forest is there in the direction the wind is carrying it? Let the foreman then give instructions to his smoke jumpers on how he will fight the fire.

3. Discuss the work that will be involved in starting a new forest.

4. Let a student visit a tree nursery to learn about the growth rate of various shade trees, fruit trees, and so on. Ask about the amount of sunlight, rain, and fertilizer they need to grow to a point where they can be safely transplanted.

5. Let a student draw pictures of a half dozen or so of the most popular lumber trees.

6. Let a student do a book report on a story about a forest fire.

7. Let a student write a diary of a smoke jumper who fights a forest fire for a single week.

MATERIALS NEEDED for LIFEPAC:

Suggested:
map of California
United States map or globe book about
Los Angeles
picture of California state flag

ADDITIONAL LEARNING ACTIVITIES

Section I *Visit to a Truck Farm*

1. Use a map of the United States and point out where California is, what lies on its orders, and what shape the state has.
2. On the same map point out the direct route from your state to California, naming the states you would travel through.
3. Collect pictures of Spanish missions and priests for an early California display.
4. Collect pictures for a display of farms being irrigated.
5. Draw and color a picture of the state flag, bird, and flower.

Section II *Trip Around the State*

1. Point out on a California map the truck farming areas.
2. Talk about the places of interest discussed in this section and find them on the map.
3. Compose a letter as a class to the chamber of commerce in a city of their choice, requesting information about places to visit. Have each child copy the class letter and send his copy to a city of his choice. Material will then return in the mail from all over California.
4. Have a group look up the names of the state and national parks in California, where they are located, and what the main attraction of each one is.
5. Another group can draw a large map of California on butcher paper. The two groups could work together to locate the parks on the map, drawing and coloring symbols for their main attractions (camping, mountains, beaches, etc.).
6. Other groups could draw scenes on large pieces of butcher paper depicting historical scenes from California (Gold Rush, missions, etc.) and display with the map.
7. If any students have visited California, have them give an oral report about their trip, show pictures, and so forth.

Section III *Work on a Truck Farm*

1. Discuss these questions with your class.
   a. Have any students ever raised carrots or lettuce? Tell how they grow and how they are picked.
   b. How are different kinds of fruit and vegetables grown and how are they harvested?
   c. How are crops irrigated?
2. Plant some lettuce seeds and watch them grow.
3. Find out how lettuce and carrots get from the fields to the stores and make pictures showing the process.
4. Find out what kinds of Indians lived in early California and draw pictures of the way they lived.

MATERIALS NEEDED for LIFEPAC:

Suggested:
felt pens: black, green, blue, yellow, and red
encyclopedia

ADDITIONAL LEARNING ACTIVITIES

Section I *Learning about Texas*

1. Use map of Texas and point out the shape of the state. Locate and discuss the panhandle, the Rio Grande, Mexico, Gulf of Mexico, and bordering states. Point out important cities.
2. Draw a map of Texas. Label important cities and rivers. Color the map.
3. Pick an important city in Texas and write a letter to the chamber of commerce requesting information about the city.
4. Make a poster showing the contributions of Texas. Cut pictures from magazines of oil, gasoline, citrus, cattle, cotton, and so forth.

Section II *Ranching in Texas*

1. Discuss the meaning of ranching and how the first cattle came into Texas. Point out the contributions missionaries made to the people in the territory of Texas. Wherever missionaries go with the Gospel, the life style of the people is improved.
2. Sing cowboy songs—"Home on the Range," "Ghost Riders in the Sky," "Get Along Little Doggie," and others.
3. Construct a model ranch. Students can bring their cows, horses, cowboys, fences, trucks, and whatever they have. (Be sure to put the child's name on each item). Buildings can be drawn or constructed of cardboard, colored and painted. The range areas could be drawn and colored on banner paper, mirrors used for water pools, Tinker Toys for windmills, and so forth.
4. Write to The Department of the Interior, Austin, Texas, 78701. Request literature on ranching in Texas.
5. Draw a picture of a trail drive. Include the wrangler, the outrider, the chuck wagon, and maybe a stampede.
6. Draw a picture of a trail drive at night. Include the night herder, the campfire, and maybe a rustler or Indians.

Section III *Rounding Up Cattle*

1. Write vocabulary for this section on the board and discuss. Pictures would increase comprehension.
2. Draw some brands on the board and discuss what they mean.
3. Discuss why cattle ranching is important, the uses of cattle, and why it is important for each rancher to brand the cattle.
4. Draw a life-size cowboy. Use a child, lying on banner paper, and trace his form. Draw in his face. One group makes his hat, another his scarf, blue jeans, chaps, boots and spurs, vest and shirt, guns, and lasso. Tape all parts to the life-size cowboy. The cowboy could also be made with real blue jeans, shirt, boots, and so forth by stuffing them full of wadded paper and running a broomstick down the back for support. Gloves make hands; a balloon, ball, or stuffed paper sack

makes the head.

5. Dramatize a roundup. Some children could be cattle in a corral, others could be the fire tender, brander, brand inspector, cowboys, and cook.

6. Have each child write down a word he has learned in this LIFEPAC. Call on a child to stand and hold his word so the whole class can see it. Then he calls on someone to explain the word. If the student responds correctly, he will have a turn to hold up his word. (This activity could also be used with questions to review before a test.)

7. Write a paragraph telling what job the student would most like to do if he were a cowboy on a ranch and why. Illustrate the paragraph.

8. Make a poster showing the ways cattle help people. Cut pictures from magazines, draw them or use brochures.

9. Draw a picture of a roundup and write a paragraph telling what is taking place in the picture.

10. Gifted students could read about and report on real cowboys of the past.

MATERIALS NEEDED for LIFEPAC:

Suggested:
map of Pennsylvania
United States map
encyclopedia

ADDITIONAL LEARNING ACTIVITIES

Section I *Facts about Coal*

1. Try to get a chunk of coal from a factory that uses it, a coal yard, or a place that sells rocks and share it with your class.
2. Show the class a diamond. Discuss how they are formed from coal.
3. Show pictures of prehistoric swamps—the beginnings of coal.
4. Discuss some by-products of coal. Make a display of pictures and items that are made from coal.
5. Draw a picture of the swamps where coal began to be formed.
6. Draw pictures or cut pictures from a magazine that show by-products of coal and make into a large poster.
7. Make a poster showing three different ways coal is used for fuel.

Section II *Methods of Coal Mining*

1. Find a book that has pictures showing historical and modern mining methods to share with your class.
2. Discuss some of the mining procedures talked about in the class.
3. Draw a simple illustration on the chalkboard of strip mining and shaft mining to show the major differences between each type of mining.
4. Draw a picture of how a coal mine would look if you could see inside the hill.

Section III *Pennsylvania—The State of Coal Mines*

1. Use a map of the United States and point out the location of Pennsylvania. Discuss its boundaries and the bordering states. Show where Pennsylvania is in relation to your state.
2. On a large map of Pennsylvania point out the rivers and how iron is brought from Erie to Pittsburgh to be made into steel. Locate the Appalachian Mountains, the state capital, and the major cities.
3. Discuss the making of the Declaration of Independence and the Liberty Bell with the class. Show them a picture of Independence Hall.
4. Draw a very large shape of Pennsylvania on banner paper, cut it out, and hang it on the wall. Draw pictures or cut pictures from magazines to show the industries or historical events of different areas. Examples: steel for Pittsburgh, a flag for Philadelphia, Hershey candy for Hershey, and so on. Play a game to see who can put the pictures on the map in the right places. (Tape rolled on the back of each picture will hold it in place.)
5. Write a short report on all the things Benjamin Franklin invented.
6. Write a short report on the famous proverbs of Benjamin Franklin.
7. Find out more about Penn's woods and William Penn.
8. Try to find some pictures of Steigel glass. Check with the finer jewelry and department stores in your city.

9. Find out about the first American flag that Betsy Ross made and draw a picture of the flag.
10. Write a letter to the Hershey Chamber of Commerce for information on how the candy is made.

MATERIALS NEEDED for LIFEPAC:

Suggested:
encyclopedia
books about Michigan

ADDITIONAL LEARNING ACTIVITIES

Section I Important Facts

1. Locate Michigan on a map. Discuss the shape, the two peninsulas, the Great Lakes, the bordering territory, and find the major cities presented in this LIFEPAC.
2. Make rice krispie treats or peanut butter chewies (see recipe on page 20).
3. Make a display of toy cars. Try to identify the make and use only those made in Detroit in the display.
4. Make a display of empty cereal boxes from the Kellogg and Post companies.
5. Collect brochures from car dealers and furniture stores for a bulletin board display.
6. Write a letter to the Kellogg or Post Company requesting brochures on how their cereal is manufactured.
7. Write a letter to the Department of Tourism, Lansing, Michigan requesting literature about their state.
8. Find out about the first "horseless carriage" and write a short report.
9. Draw a picture of Michigan's flag.

Section II Interesting People and Places

1. Take a trip to a factory that uses an assembly line.
2. Have the students write letters to the chamber of commerce in Holland, Michigan; Dearborn, Michigan; or Mackinac Island, Michigan; requesting information and pictures.
3. Draw pictures of tulips. Find illustrations in books as an example.
4. Write a short paper about Gerald Ford, or another of Michigan's native sons.

Section III Michigan Treasures

1. On a map locate the Great Lakes again, point out those lakes that border Michigan, show the St. Lawrence Seaway, and trace the route from Chicago to the ocean.
2. Discuss minerals and mining with the class.
3. Show pictures of Michigan wildlife. Discuss wildlife in your area.
4. Report on the passenger pigeon and why it is now extinct.
5. Draw a picture of the Great Lakes. Include the sea route and ships if desired.
6. Read about Hiawatha or Paul Bunyan and report to the class.

MATERIALS NEEDED for LIFEPAC:

Suggested:
four marking pens: blue, black, green,
and red
encyclopedia

ADDITIONAL LEARNING ACTIVITIES
Section I *Cape Kennedy*
1. Find Florida on a globe. Demonstrate how a rocket flies out from the earth into space.
2. Build a model space station. Construct rockets, gantries, and space capsules from cardboard, paper towel, and tissue rolls, Tinker Toys, and so forth.
3. Chart the weather for a week or two. Then pick the days that would be good for a rocket launch. The temperature, wind speed, and weather conditions (cloudy, clear) would need to be charted daily.
4. Draw and color pictures of Florida's wildlife--alligators, birds, fish, flowers, palms, and so forth. Use the encyclopedia.
5. Draw and color the Florida state flag.
6. Have each student choose a job he would like to do at the space center to help with the launch. The student could find out information about the job from the LIFEPAC, encyclopedia, and other books and give an oral report about it.

Section II *Rockets in the Sky*
1. Fly a model rocket. Be careful! Find an experienced person (older boy or girl) to help you if you have never launched one.
2. Collect pictures and make a display of rockets and satellites.
3. Let advanced students look up information and write a report about Dr. Goddard and Sir Isaac Newton and their contributions to space travel.

Section III *Space Travelers*
1. Make a chart of United States astronauts showing what they did and when.
2. Talk about mottos and their meanings. Have each student think of a good motto. Write the motto on a strip of paper from the LIFEPAC Tablet and tape it to his desk.
3. Draw a rocket and a splashdown. Name what space flight the picture shows and what astronauts are being picked up out of the water.

ADDITIONAL INFORMATION
Free materials and brochures may be obtained by writing a letter of request to
NASA
Educational Division
Cape Canaveral, Florida   32920

MATERIALS NEEDED for LIFEPAC:

Suggested:
United States map

ADDITIONAL LEARNING ACTIVITIES

Section I *California, Kansas, and Washington*

1. Ask questions of review about the industry of each state.
2. Review the location of the three states on a United States map.
3. Review the capital cities.
4. Invite a speaker. Suggested speakers are a traveler, a truck farmer or trucker who hauls for one, a farmer who uses irrigation, a wheat grower, or a native of those states.
5. Make a mural or diorama showing wheat growing, apple growing, or farm irrigation.
6. Write review questions. Exchange them and answer.
7. Collect pictures of products grown in each state. Paste them to paper and label for a poster.
8. Draw a picture of each state. Write its capital on the map and a small picture of what the state is best known for.
9. Draw the state bird, flower, and flag.

Section II *Maine, Oregon, Pennsylvania, and Texas*

See Section I of SS 310.

1. Find out about the Paul Bunyan lore and act it out or tell it to the rest of the class.
2. Find out about Davey Crockett and the battle of the Alamo. Tell it to the rest of the class.
3. Find out what happened at Independence Hall, Philadelphia, Pennsylvania, and tell the rest of the class.
4. Write a report about one of these: The national parks of Oregon, Benjamin Franklin, Sam Houston, or the Lone Star State.
5. Students draw and color a picture about the kind of work done in each state.

Section III *Florida and Michigan*

1. Review the Great Lakes and point out the St. Lawrence Seaway on the map. Show how Michigan is really an ocean port.
2. Have a rocket-building contest.
3. Construct a salt-flour map of Michigan and the Great Lakes.
4. Draw state birds, flowers, flags, and write the motto of each state across its map with the capital labeled. Present this information by oral report to the class. Then mix them all up. Have one group at a time put them together by states.
5. Write questions and answers about the nine states. Divide into two teams. Teacher asks the questions to the teams (plus some of her own for a more complete review). The team that answers the most questions wins.
6. Make Kellogg Rice Krispie marshmallow balls. Eat with Florida orange juice.
7. Collect pictures of cars made in Detroit. (Brochures from automobile dealers will help.)
8. Make a poster showing what the Great Lakes are used for – *i.e.* recreation, fishing, boating, and shipping.
9. Draw pictures of man landing on the moon.

T E S T S & K E Y S

Reproducible Tests
for use with the History &
Geography 300 Teacher's
Guide

Name _____

Write the correct answers from the list on the lines.

Penobscot	oil	traps
fog	Ma'Ama	backward
wooden	steeple	saws
five	ten	

1. Lobster pots are also called _____.

2. Herring are canned in _____.

3. A bay at Deer Isle is named _____ Bay.

4. When there is heavy _____, you cannot see ahead of you.

5. Uncle Jack put a _____ nail behind a lobster's claw.

6. Uncle Jack's boat was named the _____.

7. The church near Uncle Jack's home had a _____.

8. Granite is cut with strong _____.

9. Lobsters have _____ pairs of legs.

10. Lobsters walk _____.

Underline three words that tell what Deer Isle is famous for.

11. a. wheat   c. granite   e. lobsters

   b. herring   d. mountains   f. corn

Draw a line to match these words.

12. granite   herring

13. bluish-green   where pictures are hung

14. auction   sale

15. gallery   stone

16. sardines   lobsters

Circle the correct word.

17. Granite is cut in a _____ .

       museum   gallery   quarry

18. Inside each lobster trap is a _____ made of netting.

       funnel   barrel   marker

19. Lobsters are kept in a _____ after they are caught.

       buoy   cannery   holding tank

20. Sardines are carried along on a moving _____ at the cannery.

       tray   belt   tin

21. Uncle Jack called his house a _____ .

       hut   shack   shanty

18
___
23

Date _____

Score _____

Name _____

Write *true* or *false*.

1. _____ Judie and Paul live in Maine.

2. _____ Their grandfather lived in the west part of Kansas.

3. _____ Salt is mined in Kansas.

4. _____ Many Indian tribes once lived in Kansas.

5. _____ Combines only cut the wheat.

6. _____ Many airplanes are built in Kansas.

7. _____ David had to have an operation on his arm.

8. _____ Wee Kirk of the Valley had only six pews.

Complete these statements.

9. Judie and Paul came to Kansas on a _____.

10. The state of Kansas has many preserves for keeping

    _____ and birds.

11. The state flower of Kansas is the _____.

12. The wheat is cut and threshed by _____.

13. Red Turkey wheat is planted in the _____.

14. The church people earned money for David's

    _____.

15. Judie, Paul, and David played in the _____.

16. The farmer's crops were once eaten by _____.

17. Corn also grows in _____.

Answer each question.

18. What are the six parts of Kansas?

   a. _____   d. _____

   b. _____   e. _____

   c. _____   f. _____

19. Where is the geographical center of the United States?

   _____

20. What city is the capital of Kansas? _____

Draw a line to the right answer.

21. Soddies are made of

   a. brick
   b. glass
   c. dirt and grass

22. The mountains of Kansas are in the

   a. Pioneer section
   b. Ozark section
   c. Trails West
      section

23. A United States President was born in

   a. Dodge City
   b. Abilene
   c. Topeka

24. Judie and Paul came to Kansas on

   a. a horse
   b. a train
   c. a plane

25. Kansas is south of

   a. Nebraska
   b. Colorado
   c. Oklahoma

24 / 30

Date _____

Score _____

Name _____

Answer *true* or *false*.

1. _____ Western Washington is very wet.

2. _____ Walla Walla means *many waters*.

3. _____ Tacoma is an Indian name.

4. _____ Canada is Washington's neighbor on the east.

5. _____ The Cascade Mountains run east and west.

6. _____ Growers remove blossoms to make bigger apples.

7. _____ Apple, pear, and apricot trees blossom at the same time.

8. _____ Apples are yanked from trees.

9. _____ Pears have pockets to hold their juice.

10. _____ Apples breathe.

Draw a line to match.

11. "applesauce"   winter work in an orchard

12. "apple polisher"   south of Washington

13. pruners   river

14. Columbia   fresh apples are kept

15. Oregon   a silly remark

16. Idaho   east of Washington

17. cold room   effort to get a person to be
                              extra nice to you

Complete the lists.

18.   Name four different kinds of apples.

    a. _____

    b. _____

    c. _____

    d. _____

19.   Name five things (from winter to harvest time) **that** would ruin an apple harvest.

    a.   Failure to _____

    b.   Failure to _____

    c.   Failure to _____

    d.   Failure to _____

    e.   Failure to _____

21 / 26

Date _____

Score _____

Name _____

Write *true* or *false*.

1. _____ Volcanoes once spilled lava in Oregon.

2. _____ The Oregon Trail was made by automobiles.

3. _____ Washington borders Oregon on the north.

4. _____ Birds are enemies of the forest.

5. _____ A logging show is a play.

6. _____ A stomach robber is one who steals stomachs.

7. _____ Some paper is made from wood.

8. _____ A conifer has cones.

9. _____ Little trees are grown in a nursery.

10. _____ You can spread a log jam on your bread.

Circle the correct answer.

11. Some Douglas Fir trees may be _____ years old.

   a. 10   b. 300   c. 700

12. Enemies of the forest are _____.

   a. birds and   b. insects   c. rain and
      cats   and fire   snow

13. A pond monkey keeps the logs going in the _____.

   a. trail   b. kiln   c. river

14. Men who pull logs to the trucks are called _____.

   a. cat   b. jack   c. gopher
      skinners   monkeys   men

55

15. The man who cuts from the top of the tree is called
    _____.

    a. a cat   b. a gopher   c. an ape
       skinner   man

16. A tree that is not cut straight leaves a stump
    called a _____.

    a. gopher   b. barber   c. log jam
                        chair

Draw lines to match the words.

17. state of forests   Oregon

18. west   California and Nevada

19. east   Pacific Ocean

20. north   Washington

21. south   Idaho

Write a word from the list on each line.

        volcanoes   trimmed   log jam
        an animal   selfish   barber chair
        men   cut

22. Tree spotters say which trees are to be _____.

23. A pile-up of logs in a river is called a _____.

24. In Oregon _____ were once active.

25. A tree stump that does not cut off smoothly is

    called a _____.

26. A wolf tree is a tree that is _____.

Complete this activity.

27.   Write three things that smoke jumpers do to stop
      forest fires.

      a. _____

      b. _____

      c. _____

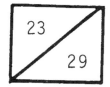

Date _____

Score _____

Name _____

Draw a line from each place to the words that go with it.

1. Los Angeles   swallows

2. Sacramento   tar pits

3. San Diego   truck farms

4. Imperial Valley   capital

5. San Francisco   zoo

6. San Juan Capistrano   Chinatown

Write the correct word on each line.

7. The country south of California is _____.

    Mexico   New Mexico   Arizona

8. The ocean to the west of California is the _____.

    Pacific Ocean   Atlantic Ocean

9. Father Serra told the Indians about _____.

    gold   Jesus   big trees

10. To bring water to fields in ditches is called

    _____.

    irrigation   mission   custom

11. People who lived on the ranch lived in a _____.

    furrow   zoo   community

12. The Indian name for the Imperial Valley was

    _____.

    Gold Place   Hollow of God's Hand

13. In California, carrots and lettuce grow during the

    _____.

    summer   winter

14. Picking vegetables by hand is called _____.

    fun   hard work   stoop labor

Write *true* or *false*.

15. _____ The All American Canal is not important to the Imperial Valley.

16. _____ A *padre* is a Spanish priest.

17. _____ *Buenos dias* means *good morning*.

18. _____ Carrots are thinned out so some plants will grow bigger.

19. _____ Mike and Terri moved to California from Kansas.

20. _____ Lettuce is packed with ice to keep it fresh.

Draw a line from the beginning of each sentence to the end.

21. The Salton Sea   are sequoia trees.

22. Many camps   go to the people in the east.

23. The biggest living   are along the ocean.
     things
                                     the furrows.

24. During irrigation,
     water moves along   pan for gold.

25. Vegetables from the   came from a river.
     west

```
┌─────────┐
│ 20  ╱   │
│   ╱  25 │
└─────────┘
```

Date _____

Score _____

Name _____

Write *true* or *false*.

1. _____ Texas is a small state.

2. _____ The Rio Grande is in north Texas.

3. _____ Austin is the capital of Texas.

4. _____ Cowboys work hard.

5. _____ A ranch is a farm that has cattle on it.

6. _____ The round**up** is a big party.

7. _____ The wrangler is the cook.

8. _____ Missionaries told the Indians about Jesus.

9. _____ Many Longhorn cattle are in Texas today.

10. _____ People go to south Texas in the winter because it is warm there.

Write a word from the list on each line.

cities   rustler   panhandle
riding circle   outrider   Mexico
Spanish   stampede   hard
Texarkana   Gulf of Mexico

11. The part of Texas that sticks up toward the north is

    called the _____.

12. The man who rides ahead on the trail drive is the

    _____.

13. When the cattle run around wildly, it is called a

    _____.

14. The water to the east of Texas is the _____

    _____.

15. Some people in west Texas speak _____.

16. The country to the south of Texas is _____.

17. One kind of cowboy who does not obey God is called

    a _____.

18. The city that is in two states is _____.

19. Ranchers sell meat from the cattle to people in

    the _____.

20. Cowboys work _____ on a ranch.

Write the correct answer on each line.

21. People use cattle for

    a. _____

    b. _____

    c. _____

22. A wrangler takes care of _____.

23. When cowboys hunt for calves on the range and bring them

    in, it is called a _____.

Draw a line to match.

24. herd   fenced in place for cattle

25. bunkhouse   made the fire for branding

26. corral   mark of the ranch

27. fire tender   taming an animal

28. rodeo   group of cattle

29. gentling   guards the cattle at night

30. night herder   house for cowboys

31. brand   a show with horses

```
 _____
|26  /      |
|   /       |
|  /    33  |
|__/_____|
```

Date _____

Score _____

Name _____

Write *true* or *false*.

1. _____ A very hard type of coal is called peat.

2. _____ Coal is a fuel.

3. _____ Bituminous coal is a soft coal.

4. _____ Coal mining today is much safer than it used to be.

5. _____ Strip mining is done under the ground.

6. _____ Erie is Pennsylvania's largest city.

Circle the correct answer.

7. Shaft mining is done _____.

    a. on the surface   b. in tunnels   c. underground

8. Coal has many _____.

    a. ashes   b. by-products   c. colors

9. The fire boss checks for _____.

    a. fires   b. gas   c. air

10. Coal is formed from _____.

    a. gases   b. oil   c. peat

11. Betsy Ross made the first American flag in _____.

    a. Hershey   b. Pittsburgh   c. Philadelphia

12. Pennsylvania is in the _____ part of the United States.

    a. eastern   b. southern   c. western

13. A city in Pennsylvania that makes candy is _____.

    a. Taffey   b. Pittsburgh   c. Hershey

Draw lines to match and then write the letters on the line.

14. _____ tunnels   a. wet land

15. _____ coal, oil, gasoline   b. passages into the earth

16. _____ swamps   c. first library

17. _____ props   d. support ceilings

18. _____ shaft mining   e. fuels

19. _____ Benjamin Franklin   f. deep in the ground

20. _____ William Penn   g. owned Pennsylvania

Write the correct answer on the line.

21. *Philadelphia* means _____.

22. The state flower of Pennsylvania is _____
_____.

23. Coal was formed years ago when trees and plants fell into
_____ and over the years became pressed together very
hard.

24. In the early coal mines, miners used a. _____ to
cut the coal from the seam, put it in b. _____,
and hoisted it out of the pits.

25. Today miners use _____ to cut the coal loose, and machines load it into railroad cars that take it out of the mines.

| 21 / 26 |

Date _____

Score _____

Name _____

Write *true* or *false*.

1. _____ Ford Motor Plant is a huge factory.

2. _____ Michigan is divided into two land parts.

3. _____ Battle Creek is known for furniture manufacturing.

4. _____ "The Old Rugged Cross" is a three-ton cross at Pokagen, Michigan.

5. _____ Michigan touches three of the Great Lakes.

6. _____ Beaver skins were sometimes used as money.

7. _____ More than a hundred historic buildings are in Greenfield Village.

8. _____ Copper is the only mineral found in Michigan.

9. _____ Holland's tulip festival begins with the scrubbing of the streets.

10. _____ Mackinac Bridge reaches to Mackinac Island.

Draw lines to match and then write the correct letters on the line.

11. _____ manufacturing

12. _____ lower peninsula

13. _____ Detroit

14. _____ horseless carriage

15. _____ assembly line

16. _____ Battle Creek

17. _____ Water Wonderland

18. _____ hymn writer

19. _____ Greenfield Village

20. _____ Mackinac Island

21. _____ a God-given treasure

a. cereal

b. summer resort

c. shaped like a mitten

d. makes automobiles

e. moving belt for manufacturing

f. lots of antiques and famous bridges

g. to make things

h. water

i. George Bennard

j. a car

k. nickname

Write a word from the Word Bank to correctly complete each sentence.

WORD BANK

smallest	airplanes	native
largest	peninsulas	ocean ships
Michigan	logging	Erie
Henry Ford	Gerald Ford	tulip
Abraham Lincoln	rose	license plates
George Bennard	furniture	bumpers

22. Michigan has two _____ .

23. Important people from a state are called _____ sons.

24. Lake Superior is the _____ of the Great Lakes.

25. The St. Lawrence Seaway makes it possible for _____ _____ to reach Michigan.

26. Lake Huron is on the thumb side of Michigan and Lake _____ is on the west side.

27. Saginaw was the _____ capital of Michigan.

28. A United States President who grew up in Grand Rapids was _____.

29. The model A was built by _____.

30. A _____ festival takes place every year in Holland, Michigan.

31. "The Great Lakes State" is written on the _____ _____ of Michigan cars.

25 / 31

Date _____

Score _____

Name _____

Answer *true* or *false*.

1. _____ The Kennedy Space Center is in Florida.

2. _____ Rockets are called "fish" by the workers.

3. _____ Alan Shepard, Jr. drove a fuel truck.

4. _____ Florida is called "The Gateway to Space."

5. _____ John Glenn was an astronaut.

6. _____ Horses, cows, and pigs live in the swamp.

7. _____ Florida is called "The Sunshine State."

8. _____ Some astronauts landed on the moon.

9. _____ The Everglades are on the moon.

10. _____ Dr. Goddard was a scientist.

Write the correct answers from the list on the lines.

rocket	Armstrong	birds
Florida	Bible	gantry
Glenn	watchtower	Sir Isaac Newton
manual		

11. Astronaut _____ was the first man to
    walk on the moon.

12. The astronauts read from the _____.

13. Technicians check the flight of the _____.

14. Many _____ live in Florida.

15. The Everglade National Park is in _____.

16. The _____ is a tower where the rocket
    is checked.

17. How a rocket works was explained by _____.

Draw lines to match and then write the correct letter on each line.

18. _____ sunshine

19. _____ rockets

20. _____ Friendship VII

21. _____ moon

22. _____ alligators

23. _____ Lake Okeechobee

24. _____ launch

25. _____ Florida

26. _____ Alan Shepard, Jr.

a. what you would see at the space center

b. live in the swamp

c. sending a rocket to space

d. a state in the United States

e. a famous astronaut

f. good weather sign

g. is in Florida

h. a very large satellite

i. John Glenn's space capsule

21 / 26

Date _____

Score _____

Name _____

Answer *true* or *false*.

1. _____ Some California cities begin with *San* which means *Saint*.

2. _____ President Eisenhower lived in Kansas as a boy.

3. _____ Portland, Maine, is close to Crater Lake.

4. _____ At Philadelphia, Pennsylvania, men signed a paper saying their country wanted to be free.

5. _____ The panhandle is part of Oregon.

6. _____ Greenfield Village has many cereal factories.

Circle the correct answer.

7. One of the greatest enemies to Oregon trees is _____.

   a lumberjack   fuel   fire

8. Washington is divided down the middle by _____.

   apples   mountains   lakes

9. Some farmers must water their crops by _____.

   irrigation   buckets   icebergs

10. Wheat seeds are usually planted in the _____.

    fall   spring   winter

11. Herring is another name for _____.

    lobster   sardines   saltfish

12. Coal takes many _____ to form.

    years   days   months

13. A man who raises cattle is a _____.

    brander   rancher   lumberjack

14. Florida weather is usually _____.

    clear and sunny   snowy and cold   rainy

15. In the Imperial Valley farmers grow _____.

    lettuce   bananas   bread

16. The geographical center of the United States is _____.

    Lebanon   Los Angeles   Austin

Draw a line to match and then write the letters on the line.

17. _____ Tallahassee   a. Oregon

18. _____ Salem   b. Washington

19. _____ Augusta   c. Florida

20. _____ Olympia   d. Maine

16 / 20

Date _____

Score _____

Notes

1. traps
2. oil
3. Penobscot
4. fog
5. wooden
6. Ma'Ama
7. steeple
8. saws
9. five
10. backward
11. b. herring
    c. granite
    e. lobsters
12. stone
13. lobsters
14. sale
15. where pictures are hung
16. herring
17. quarry
18. funnel
19. holding tank
20. belt
21. shanty

1. true
2. false
3. true
4. true
5. false
6. true
7. false
8. true
9. plane
10. animals
11. sunflower
12. combines
13. fall
14. operation
15. dugout
16. grasshoppers
17. Kansas
18. Any order:
    a. Trails West
    b. Big Lake
    c. Pioneer
    d. Frontier
    e. Wild West
    f. Ozark
19. Lebanon, Kansas
20. Topeka
21. c. dirt and grass
22. b. Ozark section
23. b. Abilene
24. c. a plane
25. a. Nebraska

1. true
2. true
3. true
4. false
5. false
6. true
7. false
8. false
9. false
10. true
11. a silly remark
12. effort to get a person to be extra nice to you
13. winter work in an orchard
14. river
15. south of Washington
16. east of Washington
17. fresh apples are kept
18. Examples; any order:
    a. Red Delicious
    b. Golden Delicious
    c. Rome Beauty
    d. Jonathan or Winesap
19. Examples; any order:
    a. thin
    b. prune
    c. pick gently
    d. keep cool after picking
    e. spray for insects

1. true
2. false
3. true
4. false
5. false
6. false
7. true
8. true
9. true
10. false
11. c
12. b
13. c
14. a
15. c
16. b
17. Oregon
18. Pacific Ocean
19. Idaho
20. Washington
21. California and Nevada
22. cut
23. log jam
24. volcanoes
25. barber chair
26. selfish
27. Any order:
    a. Using airplanes, they pour water and chemicals on the fire.
    b. Start small fires so that the big one cannot feed on them.
    c. Throw dirt on the fire.

1. tar pits
2. capital
3. zoo
4. truck farms
5. Chinatown
6. swallows
7. Mexico
8. Pacific Ocean
9. Jesus
10. irrigation
11. community
12. Hollow of God's Hand
13. winter
14. stoop labor
15. false
16. true
17. true
18. true
19. true
20. true
21. The Salton Sea came from a river.
22. Many camps are along the ocean.
23. The biggest living things are sequoia trees.
24. During irrigation water moves along the furrows.
25. Vegetables from the west go to people in the east.

1. false
2. false
3. true
4. true
5. true
6. false
7. false
8. true
9. false
10. true
11. panhandle
12. outrider
13. stampede
14. Gulf of Mexico
15. Spanish
16. Mexico
17. rustler
18. Texarkana
19. cities
20. hard
21. Examples; any order:
    a. meat
    b. hides
    c. milk
22. horses
23. roundup
24. group of cattle
25. house for cowboys
26. fenced in place for cattle
27. made the fire for branding
28. a show with horses
29. taming an animal
30. guards cattle at night
31. mark of the ranch

1. false
2. true
3. true
4. true
5. false
6. false
7. underground
8. by-products
9. gas
10. peat
11. Philadelphia
12. eastern
13. Hershey
14. b
15. e
16. a
17. d
18. f
19. c
20. g
21. brotherly love
22. Mountain Laurel
23. swamps
24. a. picks
    b. baskets or buckets
25. explosives

1. true
2. true
3. false
4. false
5. false
6. true
7. true
8. false
9. true
10. false
11. g
12. c
13. d
14. j
15. e
16. a
17. k
18. i
19. f
20. b
21. h
22. peninsulas
23. native
24. largest
25. ocean ships
26. Michigan
27. logging
28. Gerald Ford
29. Henry Ford
30. tulip
31. license plates

1. true
2. false
3. false
4. true
5. true
6. false
7. true
8. true
9. false
10. true
11. Armstrong
12. Bible
13. rocket
14. birds
15. Florida
16. gantry
17. Sir Isaac Newton
18. f
19. a
20. i
21. h
22. b
23. g
24. c
25. d
26. e

1. true
2. true
3. false
4. true
5. false
6. false
7. fire
8. mountains
9. irrigation
10. fall
11. sardines
12. years
13. rancher
14. clear and sunny
15. lettuce
16. Lebanon
17. c
18. a
19. d
20. b

ANSWER KEYS

Section One

1.1	church	1.11	stern
1.2	opera house	1.12	holding tank
1.3	general store	1.13	wharf
1.4	Answers will vary.(where, why, white, when, who, while)	1.14	buttons
		1.15	twin
1.5	Answers will vary.(please, play, plate, plant, plastic, planet)	1.16	swing
		1.17	swim
1.6	cylinder	1.18	sweet
1.7	stem	1.19	twenty
1.8	engine	1.20	twice
1.9	wheel		
1.10	bow		

Section Two

2.1	false	2.18	museum
2.2	true	2.19	auction
2.3	true	2.20	gallery
2.4	false	2.21	gallery
2.5	false	2.22	The ground is thin over the rocks.
2.6	piece	2.23	derrick
2.7	field	2.24	They are scooped up in nets.
2.8	thief	2.25	In the processing room.
2.9	niece	2.26	by a moving belt
2.10	chief	2.27	flew
2.11	the fog is thick	2.28	true
2.12	honks and whistles	2.29	glue
2.13	to help them sink	2.30	chew
2.14	by hand	2.31	due
2.15	in many places in the bay	2.32	threw
2.16	only the large lobsters	2.33	blew
2.17	auction	2.34	Drawings will vary.

Section Three

3.1	in the morning		3.16	false
3.2	they are kept in a holding tank		3.17	false
3.3	putting nails behind their joints		3.18	false
3.4	bluish-green		3.19	true
3.5	with gloves on your hands		3.20	true
3.6	cut		3.21	true
3.7	coat		3.22	false
3.8	picnic		3.23	true
3.9	can		3.24	true
3.10	candy		3.25	false
3.11	city		3.26	(say)
3.12	once		3.27	(cane)
3.13	mice		3.28	(rain)
3.14	face		3.29	(plain)
3.15	fence		3.30	(cape)

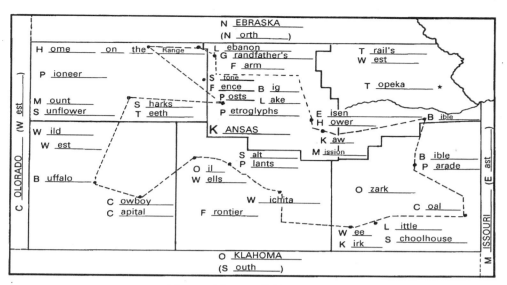

Your Map of Kansas
Map 1

Section One

1.1	see map	1.11	flat
1.2	see map	1.12	camper
1.3	plane	1.13	Trails West
1.4	Maine	1.14	Big Lake
1.5	Kansas	1.15	Pioneer
1.6	soakers	1.16	Wild West
1.7	wheat	1.17	Frontier
1.8	hail	1.18	Ozark
1.9	Red Turkey	1.19	see map
1.10	fall		

Section Two

2.1 only trails

2.2 large lakes

2.3 pioneers settled

2.4 cowboys

2.5 salt plant

2.6 mountains

2.7

Dug out	**Half-Wall**
1 door	1 door
no window	1 window
underground	part of a wall

Soddie
1 door
1 window
grass and earth
above ground

2.8	kind, child, mild, wild, mind, bind		2.14	yes
2.9	no		2.15	no
2.10	yes		2.16	no
2.11	yes		2.17	yes
2.12	yes		2.18	yes
2.13	yes			

Section Three

3.1	shrine		3.8	ocean in Kansas
3.2	shrink		3.9	preserve
3.3	sprinkle		3.10	bale
3.4	shrill		3.11	Buffalo Bill
3.5	spread		3.12	combine
3.6	spring		3.13	conservation
3.7	petroglyphs			

Section Four

4.1	dis		4.13	grasshoppers
4.2	a		4.14	elevators
4.3	in		4.15	Indian
4.4	dis		4.16	center
4.5	in		4.17	plowed
4.6	a		4.18	disks
4.7	remove water from something		4.19	harrows
4.8	the city in which the work of the state is done		4.20	fall
			4.21	winter
4.9	a machine that can cut, thresh, and bale at one time		4.22	spring
			4.23	gold
4.10	about the surface of a country		4.24	combine
4.11	Bread Basket		4.25	elevator
4.12	Dust storms		4.26	flour

Section One

1.1   Examples:
Her cheeks were as red as apples
The apple of her eye
Applesauce
Apple–pie order
An apple a day keeps the doctor away
You upset my apple cart
An apple polisher
A rotten apple

1.2   Idaho
The Pacific Ocean
Canada
Oregon

1.3   Cascade Mountains

1.4   Indian chief

1.5   many waters

1.6   the mountain

1.7   Mount Rainier

1.8   Answers will vary.

1.9   <u>scene</u>, <u>scientist</u>, <u>scissors</u>, <u>scent</u>, <u>scenery</u>

1.10   a. squeal
b. square
c. squeeze
d. squirrel
e. squawk

Section Two

2.1   false

2.2   true

2.3   false

2.4   true

2.5   false

2.6   2, 3, 1, 4

2.7   teacher check

2.8   peaches — first and second weeks in April

pears— second and third weeks in April

apricots — last week in March and first week in April

apples — last week in April or first weeks in May

2.9   The bees carry pollen on their feet.

2.10   The growers paint the blossoms with pollen.

2.11   nectar

2.12   no

2.13   The growers irrigate.

2.14   The "king" bud

2.15   five

2.16   So there will be enough food to make the remaining apples large.

2.17   from the leaves

2.18
<u>Joe</u>	<u>sold</u>	<u>crow</u>
rod	<u>hope</u>	hot
<u>stone</u>	<u>cold</u>	mop
<u>old</u>	<u>rope</u>	<u>bold</u>

2.19
beg	1	1	1
bean	2	1	1
museum	3	3	3
measure	4	2	2
neighborhood	5	3	3
science	3	2	2
refrigerator	5	5	5

Section Three

3.1 Either order:
dairy farm, chicken farm

3.2 Columbia River

3.3 Any order:
water for crops during dry times
electricity
stops flood waters
a lake for vacations

3.4 135 days

3.5 148 to 155 days

3.6 150 to 160 days

3.7 160 days

3.8 160 days

3.9 The apple has tiny pockets that hold the juice.

3.10 To keep the weight of the apples from snapping the limbs.

3.11 The center of the apple has a star–shaped pattern.

3.12 To earn money.

3.13 Machines bruise the fruit and sometimes miss apples.

3.14 The bruise turns brown and will spoil soon.

3.15 teacher check

3.16 apple juice, applesauce, jelly

3.17 2, 4, 1, 7, 3, 5, 6

3.18
ness	=	loudness
teen	=	nineteen
teen	=	fourteen
ness	=	quickness
ness	=	sadness

Section One

1.1	teacher check
1.2	teacher check
1.3	A volcano spilled out lava and then caved in.
1.4	No one knows where the water comes from.
1.5	No one knows where the water goes.
1.6	forests
1.7	lava
1.8	Douglas fir
1.9	300 feet
1.10	very wide
1.11	700
1.12	conifer

1.13	cone-bearing
1.14	Oregon Trail
1.15	fear, deer, hear, appear, cheer
1.16	un/kind, in/side, dis/close, re/read, un/true
1.17	teacher check
1.18	eat leaves
1.19	makes good lumber
1.20	is selfish
1.21	have cones
1.22	carried people
1.23	burns trees
1.24	protect trees
1.25	an important business
1.26	teacher check

Section Two

2.1	A logging show is all the work done to cut trees in the forest.
2.2	The trail blazer cuts roads into the forest.
2.3	A tree spotter decides what trees are best to cut.
2.4	A high climber cuts off short branches from tall trees.
2.5	An ape saws off the tree tops.
2.6	The stomach robber is the lumber camp cook.
2.7	slow/ly six/teen cheer/ful cup/ful friend/ship dark/ness
2.8	6, 4, 5, 3, 1, 2
2.9	moon grew soup too knew through flew

2.10	The logs are in the pond. The logs go into the mill and are sawed into strips. The strips are smoothed, dried, and graded. The poor grade lumber is ground into paper.
2.11	Examples: desks, tables, chairs, pencils
2.12	He helps get the logs into the sawmill.
2.13	pulls logs with a tractor
2.14	any lumberman
2.15	frees log jams
2.16	tin clothes
2.17	blows up log jams
2.18	picks best cut trees
2.19	fastens logs to be lifted
2.20	dries lumber

Section Three

3.1   mountainous, action, collection, joyous

3.2   Examples:
The lumbermen reseed the land.
They also plant young trees.

3.3   The plane flies over the ground and scatters seeds.

3.4   He jumps from a plane and tries to stop the fire.

3.5   They call the other spotters and the firemen.

3.6   Little trees are grown in nurseries.

3.7   Firemen use water and chemicals to put out fires.

3.8   Planes are used for reseeding the ground and putting water and chemicals on forest fires.

3.9   Wind and dry weather help to spread forest fires.

Section One

1.1   teacher check

1.2   Pacific Ocean

1.3   Oregon

1.4   Mexico

1.5   Nevada and Arizona

1.6   sigh

1.7   high

1.8   bright

1.9   light

1.10   sight

1.11   California

1.12   September

1.13   irrigation

1.14   All–American Canal

1.15   very little

1.16   furrows

1.17   top

1.18   truck farm

1.19   is another name for the Imperial Valley

1.20   is another name for priest

1.21   brought seeds to plant

1.22   grew beans and corn

1.23   is called stoop labor

1.24   teacher check

1.25   whis   per

1.26   blan   ket

1.27   moun   tain

1.28   in   deed

1.29   con   tent

Section Two

2.1 – 2.3   teacher check

2.4   El Centro

2.5   camper

2.6   San Diego

2.7   hospital

2.8   Pacific Ocean

2.9   San Juan Capistrano

2.10   The Golden Place

2.11   Jesus

2.12   Father Serra

2.13   swallows

2.14 – 2.19   teacher check

2.20   weigh

2.21   sleigh

2.22   eight

2.23 – 2.24   teacher check

2.25   cable car

2.26   Golden Gate Bridge

2.27   Chinese

2.28   customs

2.29 – 2.31   teacher check

2.32   The Golden Shore

2.33   part of San Francisco

2.34   state capital

2.35   animals found there

2.36   gold found there

2.37   fair

2.38   wear

2.39   heir

2.40   bear

2.41   pear

2.42 – 2.46   teacher check

2.47   The Salton Sea began when the Colorado River water ran into a low spot.

2.48   The Sequoia trees are big because of the way they are made. They won't burn easily.

2.49   teacher check

Section Three

3.1	good morning		3.10	no
3.2	thank you		3.11	no
3.3	vegetables		3.12	yes
3.4	4, 2, 1, 3,		3.13	yes
3.5	monkey		3.14	yes
3.6	money		3.15	(winter)
3.7	receive		3.16	(field)
3.8	key		3.17	(ice)
3.9	ceiling		3.18	(thinning)

Section One

1.1 Texas

1.2 flat grassland

1.3 raising cattle

1.4 ranches

1.5 teacher check

1.6 teacher check

1.7 teacher check

1.8 panhandle

1.9 Amarillo

1.10 ranches

1.11 Ted

1.12 meat

1.13 E/gypt

o/pen

pu/pil

stu/dent

fi/nal

i/tem

1.14 dam/age

fig/ure

thun/der

vis/it

hab/it

rob/in

1.15 teacher check

1.16 Louisiana and Arkansas

1.17 much

1.18 Texarkana

1.19 no

1.20 yes

1.21 no

1.22 no

1.23 yes

1.24 yes

1.25-1.28 teacher check

1.29 the southern edge of Texas — Rio Grande

1.30 where a river goes into a sea — mouth

1.31 winter visitors — South Texas

1.32 main South Texas city — Brownsville

1.33 truck farms — like Imperial Valley

1.34 large body of water — Gulf of Mexico

1.35-1.38 teacher check

1.39 friend's name

1.40-1.42 teacher check

1.43 fish

1.44 oil

1.45 Austin

1.46 Lyndon Johnson

1.47 Texas

1.48 Either order:

a. Dallas

b. Fort Worth

1.49 north

1.50 west

1.51 Rio Grande River

1.52 east

1.53 Examples:

Fort Worth

Dallas

Brownsville

El Paso

1.54 Example: It looks like you could pick up Texas by that part just as you might pick up a pan.

1.55 Gulf of Mexico

Section Two

2.1 Examples; Any three:

shoes

belts

hats

purses

clothing

2.2 Example: to eat

2.3 Answers will vary

2.4 cities

2.5 Longhorn

2.6 Santa Gertrudis

2.7 Any order:

a. milk

b. hides

c. meat

2.8 missionaries

2.9 3

2.10 4

2.11 2

2.12 1

2.13 Example:

Dear Lord, Thank you for helping me tell others about Jesus. Please protect me from danger that I may keep on doing your work. Help me to reach the people, bless our daily lessons. In Jesus' name, amen.

2.14 a. goodness

b. greatness

c. gentleness

d. kindness

e. largeness

f. darkness

2.15 greatness

2.16 Gentleness

2.17 kindness

2.18 largeness

2.19 <u>outrider</u>

fresh water

buffalo

good grazing land

thunder

rode ahead

<u>wrangler</u>

followed behind

six or seven horses

fresh horses

<u>night herder</u>

campfire

darkness

singing

stars

moon

2.20 Missionaries brought cattle north. They taught Indians to raise cattle.

2.21 They had to reach a town with a railroad, where the cattle were sold and shipped by train to the cities. Large trucks are used to take the cattle to the market or to the railroads.

2.22 Any four; any order:

a. stampede

b. bad weather

c. dust

d. bad water or wild buffalo, fire

2.23 The cowboys "race" around the cattle on horses trying to turn the stampeding herd into a circle, hoping to tire the cattle.

2.24 a. corny

b. fishy

c. needy

d. sticky

e. smelly

f. springy

2.25 a. (either order) joyful, thankful

b. helpful

c. playful

d. powerful

e. restful

f. harmful

g. careful

h. colorful

2.26 teacher check

2.27 teacher check

Section Three

3.1 Answers will vary

3.2 scarf

3.3 calf

3.4 self

3.5 calves

3.6 scarves

3.7 selves

3.8 gentling — taming a horse

3.9 bunkhouse — a cowboy's home

3.10 brand — burn a mark on an animal

3.11 chuck — food

3.12 rodeo — a show with horses

3.13 shoe — put metal on horses' feet

3.14 Example:

Dear Ted, I go to the Hope School. My church is little. Many people here in Pennsylvania work in factories. My dad helps to make steel. I have never ridden a horse. Please tell me what it feels like to ride a horse.

Sincerely, Tom

3.15 a. stories

b. missionaries

c. skies

d. cities

e. babies

3.16 missionaries

3.17 cities

3.18 missionary

3.19 city

3.20 sky or skies

3.21 baby, babies

3.22 stories

3.23 Any order:

a. fright

b. night

c. light

d. tight

e. sight

f. might

3.24 might

3.25 sight

3.26 Fright

3.27 night

3.28 light

3.29 tight

3.30 caught

3.31 brought

3.32 ought

3.33 taught

3.34 fought

3.35 caught or sought

3.36 thought

3.37 sought

3.38 taught

3.39 bought

3.40 teacher check

3.41 A rustler steals cattle or horses and changes the brand.

3.42 It is when the cowboys ride in different directions looking for lost cattle.

3.43 Examples:

branding

how to shoe a horse

how to gentle a horse

3.44 Across

1. Jacket

4. boots

5. scarf

Down

1. jeans

2. chaps

3. hat

3.45 a. Lazy M

b. Coffee Pot

c. Broken Arrow

d. Bar BQ

e. RB Connected

f. Little Snake

g. Rocking R

3.46 Drawings will vary; teacher check

3.47 Drawings will vary; teacher check

Section One

1.1 a.   4

      b.   2

      c.   5

      d.   1

      e.   3

Dead trees and plants were the beginnings of coal. Dead trees and plants fall into swamps. A wet, wood-like peat formed from dead trees and plants. Soil presses water from peat. Coal was formed from peat.

1.2 C

      O

      A

      L

1.3 (oil) (twigs) (gasoline) (hay) (straw) (newspaper)

1.4 a.   ie

      b.   ie

      c.   ei

      d.   ei

      e.   ie

      f.   ie

      g.   ie

1.5 believe

1.6 piece

1.7 niece

1.8 receive

1.9 ceiling

1.10 field

1.11 chief

1.12 anthracite

1.13 bituminous

1.14 anthracite

1.15 anthracite

1.16 bituminous

1.17 anthracite

1.18 bituminous

1.19 spongy beginning of coal — peat

1.20 anything that burns — fuel

1.21 hard coal — anthracite

1.22 something made from coal — by-product

1.23 soft coal — bituminious

1.24 wet land — swamp

Section Two

2.1 Example: coloring

2.2 Example: to water

2.3 Example: he got rich

2.4 Example: poles or tall sticks to hold something up

2.5 Example: does not hold something against

2.6 true

2.7 false

2.8 true

2.9 true

	Years Ago	Today
2.10	candles	
2.11		electricity
2.12	picks and shovels	
2.13		machines
2.14		explosives
2.15		safety lamps

	Years Ago	Today
2.16		fans
2.17		steel supports
2.18	no supports	
2.19		telephones
2.20	no way to call for help	
2.21		water lines
2.22	many fires	
2.23	many explosions	
2.24	many cave-ins	
2.25	poor health	
2.26		fire boss
2.27	felt	
2.28	built	
2.29	wilt	

2.30 belt

2.31 quilt

2.32 melt

2 33 halt

2.34 salt

2.35 Shaft mining is mining deep into the ground. Strip mining is mining close to the surface of the earth.

2.36 The "streets" are tunnels dug to mine more coal.

2.37 a. Strip mining is the safest kind of mining.

b. Strip mining spoils the beauty of the land.

2.38 "Yea, the darkness hideth not from thee; but the night shineth as the day; the darkness and the light are both alike to thee."

Section Three

3.1 teacher check

3.2 teacher check

3.3 teacher check

3.4 teacher check

3.5 teacher check

3.6 teacher check

3.7 Answers will vary

3.8 b. Penn was fair to the Indians

3.9 a. started the first library in America

3.10 c. made glassware

3.11 b. brotherly love

3.12 b. gave land to William Penn

3.13 a. bifocals

3.14 teacher check

3.15 teacher check

3.16 teacher check

3.17 grudge

3.18 bridge

3.19 pledge

3.20 judge, judge

3.21 budge

3.22 hedge

Section One

1.1 f

1.2 e

1.3 b

1.4 d

1.5 a

1.6 g

1.7 false

1.8 false

1.9 true

1.10 false

1.11 true

1.12 true

1.13 true

1.14 liking

1.15 arriving

1.16 becoming

1.17 realizing

1.18 making

1.19 shining

1.20 living

1.21 believing

1.22 Canada

1.23 four

1.24 Ford

1.25 cars

1.26 Michigan

1.27 cherries

1.28 Traverse City

1.29 helper check

1.30 helper check

1.31 mitten

1.32 thumb

1.33 peninsula

1.34 bird

1.35 Either order:

    a. upper

    b. lower

1.36 Straits of Mackinac

1.37 factory

1.38 cherries

1.39 peninsulas

1.40 mitten

1.41 longest

1.42 five

1.43 strong

1.44 cables

1.45 grinning

1.46 hopping

1.47 fannlng

1.48 beginning

1.49 trapping

1.50 spinning

1.51 sunning

1.52 batting

1.53 a. manufacturing

    b. nicknames

    c. cars

    d. cereal

    e. furniture

1.54 Examples:

    <u>Kellogg Company</u>

    a. Rice Krispies

    b. Corn Flakes

    c. Sugar Smacks

    d. Fruit Loops

Post Company

    a.   Post Toasties

    b.   Grape Nut Flakes

    c.   Sugar Crisp

    d.   Alpha Bits

1.55   teacher check

1.56   e

1.57   f

1.58   d

1.59   b

1.60   c

1.61   Any order:

    a.   Battle Creek

    b.   Grand Rapids

    c.   Detroit

1.62   Any order:

    a.   cereal

    b.   furniture

    c.   cars

1.63   Any order:

    a.   Ford

    b.   Chevrolet

    c.   Oldsmobile

    d.   Buick or Pontiac

1.64   Henry Ford

1.65   "Horseless Carriages"

1.66   c

1.67   e

1.68   a or b

1.69   b or d

1.70   d or a

1.71   teacher check

1.72   teacher check

Section Two

2.1   teacher check

2.2   a.   pŭd/dle

    b.   tā/ble

    c.   bŭn/dle

    d.   ăn/kle

    e.   Bī/ble

    f.   hŭd/dle

2.3   a.   ta/ble

    b.   pud/dle

    c.   rat/tle

    d.   nee/dle

    e.   can/dle

2.4   a Ford

2.5   Model T

2.6   Ford Motor Company

2.7   on a farm near Dearborn, Michigan

2.8   machines and engines

2.9   the Ford Motor Company

2.10   cars

2.11   eight hundred fifty dollars

2.12   six hundred dollars

2.13   more

2.14   an assembly line

2.15   shorter

2.16   helper check

2.17   Henry

2.18   President

2.19   native

2.20   football

2.21   leader

2.22 a. purest

b. simplest

c. safest

d. bluest

e. truest

f. freest

g. largest

h. finest

2.23 a. batter

b. sitter

c. fatter

d. trapper

e. flatter

f. spinner

g. beginner

h. bidder

2.24 Dutch

2.25 canal

2.26 living

2.27 tulips

2.28 festival

2.29 Dutch

2.30 scrub

2.31 Henry Ford

2.32 history

2.33 antiques

2.34 Greenfield Village

2.35 Thomas Edison

2.36 more than one hundred

2.37 country

2.38 a.

b. ✓

c.

d. ✓

e.

f. ✓

g. ✓

h. ✓

i. ✓

2.39 e. antiques — old things

2.40 c. Greenfield Village — more than one hundred buildings from history

2.41 g. Abraham Lincoln — bloodstained chair

2.42 f. Martha-Mary Church — named after mothers of Ford and his wife

2.43 a. William H. McGuffey — readers

2.44 d. Tin Lizzie — built by Henry Ford

2.45 b. Thomas Edison — inventor

2.46 true

2.47 false

2.48 false

2.49 true

2.50 false

2.51 true

2.52 false

2.53 true

2.54 true

2.55 false

2.56 true

2.57 true

2.58 false

2.59 false

2.60 a. 1. Greenfield

b. 2. Detroit

c. 3. tourists

d. 4. Straits

e. 5. scrub

f. 6. Battle Creek

g. 7. Kellogg

2.61	teacher check	2.67	d
2.62	teacher check	2.68	b
2.63	c	2.69	e
2.64	b	2.70	c
2.65	a	2.71	d
2.66	e		

Section Three

3.1 Lake Ontario

3.2 Lake Erie

3.3 Either order:

    a.   Lake Michigan

    b.   Lake Huron

3.4 Lake Superior

3.5 Lake Huron

3.6 Lake Superior

3.7 teacher check

3.8 Either order:

    a.   The Great Lakes State

    b.   Water Wonderland

3.9 Any order:

    a.   It is deep. It is busy.

    b.   People vacation on sandy beaches.

    c.   Sailboats and big boats use it. It can be dangerous.

3.10 Any order:

    a.   Lake Huron

    b.   Lake Michigan

    c.   Lake Erie

    d.   Lake Superior

3.11 Lake Ontario

3.12 Lake Superior

3.13 Either order:

    a.   Lake Huron

    b.   Lake Michigan

3.14 Great Lake

3.15 Either order:

    a.   Lake Superior

    b.   Lake Huron

3.16 Either order:

    a.   St. Claire River

    b.   Detroit River

3.17 yes

3.18 yes

3.19 teacher check

3.20 true

3.21 true

3.22 false

3.23 false

3.24 false

3.25 false

3.26 true

3.27 true

3.28 true

3.29 true

3.30 d. Lake Superior — largest of the Great Lakes

3.31 h. St. Lawrence Seaway — brings ocean ships to Michigan

3.32 e. "Michi" — great

3.33 f. beaver — much wanted fur

3.34 g. St. Mary's River — joins two Great Lakes

3.35 c. lore — stories

3.36 a. Lake Michigan — deep and busy

3.37 b. fur trade — very good for awhile

3.38 beaver furs

3.39 jewels

3.40 tough

3.41 rich

3.42 logging

3.43 wrong

3.44 logs

3.45 disappeared

3.46 a.   bread
b.   lead
c.   read
d.   dead
e.   tread
f.   breath

3.47 Either order:
a.   wreath
b.   neat

3.48 a

3.49 copper

3.50 magnetic (iron) ore

3.51 salt

3.52 iron (magnetic iron ore)

3.53 oil and natural gas

3.54 Any order:
a.   copper
b.   iron

c.   coal
d.   salt
e.   oil or peat, natural gas

3.55 true

3.56 false

3.57 true

3.58 false

3.59 false

3.60 true

3.61 true

3.62 true

3.63 b.   much wildlife

3.64 c.   almost everywhere in Michigan

3.65 b.   extinct

3.66 a.   protected by law

3.67 teacher check

3.68 robin

3.69 a.   1. Model T or A
b.   2. Bridge
c.   3. cereal
d.   4. Huron
e.   5. furniture
f.   6. passenger
g.   7. Automobile
h.   8. peninsulas
i.   9. Michigan

3.70 teacher check

3.71 teacher check

3.72 teacher check

3.73 teacher check

Section One

1.1   The state motto is "In God We Trust."

1.2   The birds and animals are safe in the Everglades National Park.

1.3   A swamp is wet, soft land covered with grass growing in water. The Everglades area is a swamp.

1.4   no

1.5   yes

1.6   no

1.7   yes

1.8   yes

1.9   teacher check

1.10-1.11 Examples:

1.10   The space center was built in Florida because of flat beaches and good weather.

1.11   The Everglades is a wet place covered with grass. Alligators and birds live there.

1.12   Swanee River

1.13   mockingbird

1.14   Everglades

1.15   beaches

1.16   Cape Canaveral

1.17   lakes

1.18   grass

1.19   alligators

1.20   space

1.21   weather

1.22   lake

1.23   storm

1.24   State

1.25   snakes

1.26   Cape

1.27   safe

1.28   lake

1.29   place

1.30   controls

1.31   checked

1.32   windows

1.33   rocket

1.34   fuel

1.35   e   scientists — study about space

1.36   a   truck drivers — bring the fuel

1.37   b   engineers — plot a path for the rocket

1.38   f   weathermen — watch for storms

1.39   c   technicians — watch the rocket on a screen

1.40   g   gantry workers — move the tower to the parking area

1.41   d   builders — put up towers and buildings

Section Two

2.1   c   missile — is another word for rocket

2.2   d   Dr. Goddard — was a scientist from the United States

2.3   a   fireworks — can be very dangerous

2.4   e   bombs — destroyed buildings

2.5   b   Sir Isaac Newton — explained how a rocket works

2.6 a. (missile)
     b. (shoot)
     c. (satellite)
     d. (world)
     e. (coast)
     f. (follow)
     g. (work)
     h. (find)
     i. (part)
     j. (place)

2.7 no

2.8 no

2.9 yes

2.10 no

2.11 yes

2.12 launches

2.13 satellites

2.14 lakes

2.15 matches

2.16 recesses

2.17 churches

2.18 fixes

2.19 scientists

2.20 flashes

2.21 blesses

2.22 alligators

Section Three

3.1 a. sent
     b. cent
     c. sales
     d. sails
     e. Do
     f. due
     g. tail
     h. tale

3.2 Alan Shepard

3.3 Friendship VII

3.4 ocean

3.5 jet

3.6 Kennedy

3.7 The word astronaut means space traveler.

3.8 because they traveled into space

3.9 People thought they might find monsters in space, and the moon made of green cheese.

3.10 Some people were afraid of space because they did not understand it.

3.11 Example: I am frightened of the dark and of things I might see in the dark. I am afraid of seeing eyes looking at me in the dark.

3.12 yes

3.13 yes

3.14 yes

3.15 no

3.16 no

3.17 yes

3.18 Any order:
      a. White
      b. Grissom
      c. Chaffee

3.19 Any order:
      a. Borman
      b. Lovell
      c. Anders

3.20 The astronauts remembered God by

reading from the Bible (Genesis 1:1-10).

3.21
a. space craft
b. block house
c. weather man
d. fire works
e. air plane
f. Everglades
g. man kind
h. broad cast
i. some time
j. gate way
k. mockingbird

3.22 Canaveral

3.23 moon

3.24 Saturn V

3.25 Apollo XI

3.26 Armstrong

3.27 Tranquility Base

3.28 teacher check

3.29
a. cen ter
b. roc ket
c. mot to
d. con trol
e. sun ny
f. cap sule
g. mes sage
h. com mand
i. es cape
j. prac tice

Section One

1.1 (valley)

1.2 (carrots)

1.3 (irrigation)

1.4 (fertilizer)

1.5 (eighty)

1.6 (plow)

1.7 fall

1.8 mills

1.9 elevators

1.10 summer

1.11 golden

1.12 (hail)

(hard rains)

1.13 false

1.14 true

1.15 false

1.16 false

1.17 true

1.18 false

1.19 true

1.20 true

1.21 true

1.22 (crops)

(combine)

(machines)

(bees)

(trucks)

(people)

1.23 San Francisco — Chinatown

1.24 Abilene — President Eisenhower

1.25 Lebanon — geographical center

1.26 Walla Walla — many waters

1.27 Sacramento — capital city of California

1.28 Seattle — Indian chief

1.29 Los Angeles — largest city in California

1.30 San Juan Capistrano — Spanish mission

1.31 Topeka — capital city of Kansas

1.32 Olympia — capital city of Washington

Section Two

2.1 (Maine)

2.2 (traps and nets)

2.3 (Maine)

2.4 (Maine)

2.5 (northeastern)

2.6 (sink)

2.7 (sardines)

2.8 (bottom)

2.9 (rocks and fog)

2.10 4

2

1

3

2.11 Any order:

a. insects

b. leaf-eating worms

c. wolf trees

d. fire

2.12   Any order:

   a.   ape

   b.   trailblazer

   c.   tree spotter or high climber, choppers

2.13   teacher check

2.14   false

2.15   false

2.16   true

2.17   true

2.18   false

2.19   true

2.20   false

2.21   true

2.22   true

2.23   false

2.24   false

2.25   teacher check

2.26   teacher check

2.27   teacher check

2.28   Christopher Columbus — brought cattle to America

2.29   branding — tells the cow's owner

2.30   hides — used to make handbags

2.31   flat grassland — grazing land

2.32   history — stories of the past

2.33   cattle drive — walking the cattle to market

2.34   Portland

2.35   Oklahoma

2.36   Austin

2.37   Pennsylvania

2.38   Oregon

2.39   President

2.40   Oregon

2.41   capital

2.42   The town is located as far east as one could travel.

Section Three

3.1   Check; flat, sandy beaches, an ocean nearby, good weather

3.2   scientists

   truck drivers

   weathermen

   astronauts

   engineers

3.3   Cape Canaveral, Florida

3.4   Gulf of Mexico

3.5   astronaut

3.6   Atlantic Ocean

3.7   Tallahassee

3.8   Lansing

3.9   Automobile Capital

3.10   Tower

3.11   Henry Ford

3.12   Great Lakes

3.13   history

3.14   Example: Michigan has four times as much water as any other state. Michigan touches all but one of the five Great Lakes.

3.15   Example: Greenfield Village has Henry Ford's collections. They are old American homes, stores, and other buildings from all over the U.S.

3.16   Example: Henry Ford used an assembly line. Each workman did one job over and over again.

3.17   California

3.18   Florida

3.19   Oregon

3.20   Michigan

3.21   Texas

3.22   Pennsylvania

3.23   Maine

3.24   Washington

3.25   Kansas

3.26   teacher check

3.27   south

3.28   north

3.29   west

3.30   west

3.31   east

3.32   west

Notes

Self Test 1

1.01	false		1.016	back
1.02	true		1.017	stone
1.03	true		1.018	brother and sister
1.04	false		1.019	uncle
1.05	true		1.020	lobster trap
1.06	false		1.021	Deer Isle
1.07	true		1.022	Maine
1.08	true		1.023	yellow
1.09	true		1.024	lobster fishing
1.010	false		1.025	wheel
1.011	town		1.026	shanty
1.012	fish		1.027	wharf
1.013	front		1.028	lobster
1.014	Uncle Jack's boat		1.029	general
1.015	state		1.030	lobster fishing

Self Test 2

2.01 Deer Isle

2.02 morning

2.03 sauce

2.04 Iowa

2.05 rocks

2.06 shanty

2.07 bottom

2.08 Maine

2.09 Sardines

2.010 funnels

2.011
granite — stone
auction — led by a man
sardines — fish
lobster traps — pots
Deer Isle — island
scoop — to pick up
general store — many things to buy
museum — old things

Ma'Ama — boat
gallery — pictures

2.012 c. X fish

2.013 c. X stone

2.014 b. X a sale

2.015 c. X fish

2.016 true

2.017 true

2.018 true

2.019 false

2.020 true

2.021 false

2.022 true

2.023 false

2.024 true

2.025 false

Self Test 3

3.01	false		3.016	cooked lobster
3.02	true		3.017	to help
3.03	true		3.018	wooden
3.04	true		3.019	live lobster
3.05	false		3.020	over
3.06	false		3.021	bluish green
3.07	true		3.022	red
3.08	true		3.023	bridge
3.09	true		3.024	shells
3.010	true		3.025	stalks
3.011	hard shelled		3.026	cannery
3.012	sardines		3.027	gloves
3.013	granite		3.028	thank you
3.014	sale		3.029	gallery
3.015	Iowa		3.030	learned

Self Test 1

1.01	Maine	1.014	Nebraska
1.02	Kansas	1.015	Oklahoma
1.03	by plane	1.016	false
1.04	camper	1.017	true
1.05	Red Turkey	1.018	false
1.06	Trails West	1.019	true
1.07	Big Lake	1.020	false
1.08	Pioneer	1.021	false
1.09	Wild West	1.022	false
1.010	Frontier	1.023	false
1.011	Ozark	1.024	false
1.012	Colorado	1.025	true
1.013	Missouri		

Self Test 2

2.01	X b. caves	2.014	false
2.02	X a. soil and grass	2.015–2.020 any order:	
2.03	X c. the center of the parts of the United States that touch	2.015	Trails West
		2.016	Big Lakes
2.04	X a. storm clouds	2.017	Pioneer
2.05	X c. to Kansas	2.018	Wild West
2.06	true	2.019	Frontier
2.07	false	2.020	Ozark
2.08	true	2.021	Kansas
2.09	true	2.022	above
2.010	true	2.023	flat
2.011	true	2.024	Kansas
2.012	false	2.025	Red
2.013	false		

Self Test 3

3.01	T	3.011	Lebanon
3.02	T	3.012	soddies
3.03	T	3.013	preserves
3.04	F	3.014	clay tablets
3.05	F	3.015	farms and lakes
3.06	cowboys	3.016	Mount Sunflower
3.07	sunflower	3.017	cowboys
3.08	wheat	3.018	salt plants
3.09	Dodge City	3.019	strip mining
3.010	Topeka	3.020	Answers will vary.

Self Test 4

4.01	false	4.013	caves
4.02	true	4.014	state flower
4.03	false	4.015	cowboy capital
4.04	false	4.016	mill
4.05	true	4.017	gold
4.06	true	4.018	elevators
4.07	false	4.019	grass
4.08	true	4.020	Trucks
4.09	true	4.021	picture
4.010	machine	4.022	Topeka
4.011	state	4.023	coal
4.012	center of the parts of the United States that touch	4.024	Red Turkey
		4.025	Harvest

Self Test 1

1.01	Washington		1.014	False
1.02	Columbia		1.015	True
1.03	Pacific		1.016	Apples are good for you.
1.04	Wenatchee		1.017	He is bad.
1.05	Seattle		1.018	You spoiled my plan.
1.06	Rainier		1.019	That remark is silly.
1.07	Canada		1.020	You try to get people to be extra nice to you.
1.08	Idaho			
1.09	Cascade		1.021	They had food ready for them.
1.010	Oregon			They washed their car.
1.011	False			Many people came to the party.
1.012	True			They put up a welcome sign.
1.013	False			They had a party for them.
				They painted the house.
				They thanked God for the Sanders.

Self Test 2

2.01	true		2.014	clusters
2.02	true		2.015	king
2.03	false		2.016	People
2.04	true		2.017	welcoming
2.05	true		2.018	Seattle
2.06	true		2.019	So he will get larger apples.
2.07	true		2.020	The Cascade Mountains stop it.
2.08	false		2.021	The trees would die.
2.09	pruners		2.022	no
2.010	sprayed		Examples:	
2.011	Codling		2.023	Seattle
2.012	Grand Coulee		2.024	Walla Walla
2.013	rose		2.025	Tacoma

Self Test 3

3.01   Pacific Ocean

3.02   Canada

3.03   Idaho

3.04   Oregon

3.05   gives electricity

3.06   gives vacation place

3.07   prevents floods

3.08   stores water for dry times

3.09–3.015 any order:

3.09   pruners

3.010   pickers

3.011   sorters

3.012   blossom trimmers

3.013   washer-rinsers

3.014   packers

Note: a question has been added to this Self Test. Follow the set of answers which match the LIFEPAC being graded.

3.015	false	–	pollen painters
3.016	true	–	false
3.017	true	–	true
3.018	true	–	true
3.019	true	–	true
3.020	true	–	true
3.021	true	–	true
3.022	true	–	true
3.023	Jonathans	–	true
3.024	Red Delicious	–	Jonathans

3.025	Golden Delicious	–	Red Delicious
3.026	Winesaps	–	Golden Delicious
3.027	a dam	–	Winesaps
3.028	a river	–	a dam
3.029	mountains	–	a river
3.030	a city	–	mountains
3.031		–	a city

Self Test 1

1.01	no		1.011	state
1.02	yes		1.012	lava
1.03	no		1.013	10-feet wide
1.04	no		1.014	cones
1.05	yes		1.015	eat leaves
1.06	yes		1.016	selfish
1.07	no		1.017	west
1.08	yes		1.018	700
1.09	yes		1.019	insects and fire
1.010	yes		1.020	Idaho

Self Test 2

2.01	falling		2.014	yes
2.02	cut		2.015	yes
2.03	log jam		2.016	no
2.04	lumber		2.017	no
2.05	rings		2.018	yes
2.06	volcanoes		2.019	no
2.07	selfish		2.020	yes
2.08	sawmill		2.021	cuts top of tree off
2.09	barber chair		2.022	cuts branches
2.010	branches		2.023	says what trees are to be cut
2.011	no		2.024	cuts roads
2.012	yes		2.025	gets logs into mill
2.013	no			

Self Test 3

3.01	yes		3.08	Oregon
3.02	no		3.09	cat skinners
3.03	yes		3.010	smoke jumpers
3.04	no		3.011	rings
3.05	yes		3.012	water
3.06	no		3.013	gopherman
3.07	jack monkeys		3.014	ape

3.015   barber chair
3.016   Oregon
3.017   Pacific Ocean

3.018   Idaho
3.019   Washington
3.020   California and Nevada

Self Test 1

1.01	no		1.011	grows vegetables to sell
1.02	yes		1.012	furrows
1.03	no		1.013	September
1.04	yes		1.014	Hollow of God's Hand
1.05	no		1.015	irrigation
1.06	no		1.016	lettuce
1.07	no		1.017	Arizona and Nevada
1.08	yes		1.018	Pacific Ocean
1.09	picking crops by hand		1.019	Mexico
1.010	a priest		1.020	Oregon

Self Test 2

2.01	no		2.014	Father Serra
2.02	yes		2.015	sequoia trees
2.03	yes		2.016	ranch
2.04	yes		2.017	were called padres
2.05	yes		2.018	traveled in a camper
2.06	no		2.019	called the land Kun Shan
2.07	no		2.020	are grown
2.08	yes		2.021	goes along the furrows
2.09	The Golden Place		2.022	is the state capital
2.010	San Juan Capistrano		2.023	They built missions to have places to tell the Indians about Jesus.
2.011	Pacific Ocean		2.024	Answers will vary.
2.012	El Centro		2.025	They get water from the All–American Canal.
2.013	lettuce			

Self Test 3

3.01	Spanish	3.016	must be thinned
3.02	carrots and lettuce	3.017	yes
3.03	the Colorado River	3.018	yes
3.04	Sacramento	3.019	yes
3.05	The Golden Place	3.020	no
3.06	sequoia trees	3.021	yes
3.07	vegetables	3.022	no
3.08	Mexico	3.023	yes
3.09	irrigation	3.024	La Brea Tar Pits
3.010	El Centro	3.025	zoo
3.011	is stoop labor	3.026	Chinatown and cable cars
3.012	is a priest	3.027	All-American Canal
3.013	was the Hollow of God's Hand	3.028	strange lake
3.014	is at San Juan Capistrano	3.029	The valley has lots of sun and water.
3.015	means The Golden Shore	3.030	Answers will vary

Self Test 1

1.01 cotton   oil
1.02 Dallas   Fort Worth
1.03 warm   sunny
1.04 on top of   a figure
a mountain
1.05 swim   sunbathe
1.06 Louisiana   Arkansas
1.07 Arkansas   Texas
1.08 has ranching land
is in north Texas

1.09 Mexico
1.010 South
1.011 largest
1.012 Spanish
1.013 mouth
1.014 ranch
1.015 Austin
1.016 Rio Grande
1.017 panhandle

Self Test 2

2.01 sell
2.02 clothing
2.03 to tell Indians of Jesus
2.04 Oklahoma
2.05 he gave the cowboys fresh horses
2.06 north Texas
2.07 Mexico
2.08 about Jesus
2.09 raise cattle themselves

2.010 sell the cattle
2.011 guard the cattle
2.012 Texarkana
2.013 oil
2.014 raising cattle to sell
2.015 a stampede
2.016 mouth
2.017 Austin
2.018 rode ahead of the herd

Self Test 3

3.01 running away
3.02 cattle farm
3.03 food
3.04 skin
3.05 cowboy house
3.06 contest for cowboys
3.07 to quiet down
3.08 north Texas
3.09 capital of Texas
3.010 kept the horses
3.011 dangerous

3.012 yes
3.013 no
3.014 no
3.015 yes
3.016 no
3.017 no
3.018 no
3.019 yes
3.020 no
3.021 no

3.022	corral		a show with horses
3.023	brand		the mark on a cow to show who owns it
3.024	chaps		training a horse so it is easy to manage
3.025	rodeo		a fenced yard in which to put cattle and horses
3.026	gentling		worn to protect the cowboys' legs
3.027	missionaries		looked for grazing land
3.028	Texarkana		raising cattle to sell
3.029	outrider		told Indians about Jesus
3.030	oil		in two states
3.031	ranching		grown in Texas
			found in Texas

Self Test 1

1.01 (fuel)

1.02 (energy)

1.03 (peat)

1.04 (anthracite)

1.05 (wet land)

1.06 Example: Trees and plants die and fall into the swamp. Peat forms from these dead plants and gets hard as more soil forms on top of it.

1.07 Example: Coal is important for heat and for energy.

1.08 by-product

1.09 fuel

1.010 swamps

1.011 factories

1.012 coal

1.013 oil, natural gas, coal — fuels used to make energy

1.014 energy — used to run machinery

1.015 factories — places for making things

1.016 bituminous — soft coal

1.017 fuel — anything that burns

1.018 (burn), (dry out)

1.019 (our bodies) (machines)

1.020 (bituminous) (anthracite)

Self Test 2

2.01 false

2.02 false

2.03 true

2.04 false

2.05 true

2.06 true

2.07 false

2.08 true

2.09 true

2.010 fuel — makes energy

2.011 strip mining — mining on the surface of the land

2.012 tunnels — passages into the earth

2.013 anthracite — hard coal

2.014 coal, gasoline, oil — fuels

2.015 poor lighting — electric lights

2.016 cave-ins — steel props

2.017 explosions of gas — a fire boss

2.018 (underground)

2.019 (rock)

2.020 (by-products)

Self Test 3

3.01   false

3.02   true

3.03   false

3.04   true

3.05   true

3.06   true

3.07   bifocals

3.08   chocolate

3.09   eastern

3.010 Philadelphia

3.011 Independence Hall

3.012 England

3.013 Independence

3.014 glassware

3.015 Benjamin Franklin

3.016 soft

3.017 anthracite

3.018 shaft mining

3.019 Any one of these:
       medicine, gases, tars, heat,
       man-made rubber, fertilizers,
       food dyes, or bug sprays

3.020 props (supports)

Self Test 1

1.01 h manufacture — make things

1.02 i factory — Ford Motor Plant

1.03 j inspector — checks things

1.04 b lower peninsula — shaped like a mitten

1.05 k Straits of — water between the Mackinac peninsulas

1.06 g engineer — plans engines

1.07 c Mackinac Bridge — joins the peninsulas

1.08 f cereal — Battle Creek

1.09 d automobiles — Detroit

1.010 e tool and die maker — makes tools

1.011 a furniture — Grand Rapids

1.012 false

1.013 true

1.014 true

1.015 true

1.016 true

1.017 false

1.018 false

1.019 true

1.020 false

1.021 true

1.022 false

1.023 false

1.024 true

1.025 true

1.026 Any order:

    a.   Detroit

    b.   Grand Rapids

    c.   Battle Creek

1.027 Any order:

    a.   cereal

    b.   furniture

    c.   cars

1.028 Any order:

    a.   Ford

    b.   Buick

    c.   Chevrolet

        or Oldsmobile, Pontiac

1.029 Either order:

    a.   upper peninsula

    b.   lower peninsula

1.030 Either order:

    a.   Kellogg Company

    b.   Post Company

1.031 The Great Lakes State

Self Test 2

2.01 false

2.02 true

2.03 false

2.04 true

2.05 false

2.06 false

2.07 false

2.08 true

2.09 true

2.010 true

2.011 true

2.012 f shaped like a mitten — lower peninsula

2.013 e "The Old Rugged Cross" — Reverend George Bennard

2.014 c Mackinac Island — resort

2.015 h Greenfield Village — many old buildings

2.016 a Gerald Ford — President

2.017 b Grand Rapids — furniture

2.018 i Battle Creek — cereal

2.019 j cherries — Traverse City

2.020 d Thomas Edison — famous inventor

2.021 g Model A — Henry Ford

2.022 four

2.023 manufactures

2.024 cars

2.025 tower

2.026 a. factory

b. assembly line

2.027 a. cereal

b. Battle Creek

2.028 peninsulas

2.029 license plates

2.030 hardwoods

2.031 festival

2.032 hymn

2.033 Examples; any order:

a. Greenfield Village

b. Holland, Michigan

c. Mackinac Island

Self Test 3

3.01 false

3.02 false

3.03 true

3.04 true

3.05 false

3.06 true

3.07 true

3.08 true

3.09 true

3.010 true

3.011 true

3.012 cereal

3.013 furniture

3.014 mitten

3.015 factory

3.016 native sons

3.017 President

3.018 a. minister

b. hymn

3.019 logging

3.020 God

3.021 surveyor

3.022 extinct

3.023 apple blossom

3.024 Examples: Gerald Ford was President of the United States. Henry Ford made cars on an assembly line. George Bennard wrote "The Old Rugged Cross."

3.025 Example: Water

It is used for fishing, vacations, and boating. The Great Lakes join together to make a waterway to the ocean.

3.026 Either order:

a. upper peninsula

b.   lower peninsula

3.027 Any order:

    a.   The Great Lakes State

    b   Wolverine State

    c.   Automobile Capital of the World or Water Wonderland

3.028 Any order:

    a.   Detroit

    b.   Battle Creek

    c.   Grand Rapids

3.029 Any order:

    a.   cereal

    b.   automobiles

    c.   furniture

3.030 Any order:

    a.   Ford

    b.   Buick

    c.   Oldsmobile or Pontiac, Chevrolet

3.031 Any order:

    a.   water

    b.   minerals

    c.   wildlife

    d.   fur or forests

3.032 Any order:

    a.   Lake Erie

    b.   Lake Michigan

    c.   Lake Huron

    d.   Lake Superior

3.033 k   passenger pigeon — extinct

3.034 g   engineer — plans and makes engines

3.035 i   Ford Motor Plant — factory that makes cars

3.036 d   Grand Rapids — furniture

3.037 f   lower peninsula — shaped like a mitten

3.038 a   Gerald Ford — President

3.039 l   St. Lawrence Seaway — waterway from Great Lakes to ocean

3.040 j   Model A — first Ford car

3.041 h   Battle Creek — cereal

3.042 c   Saginaw — logging capital

3.043 e   lumberjacks — hard, tough men

3.044 b   "Michi" — means "great"

Self Test 1

1.01	sunny	
1.02	Canaveral	
1.03	Sunshine	
1.04	rockets	
1.05	e	Cape — Canaveral
1.06	a	space — center
1.07	d	gantry — tower
1.08	c	rocket — fuel
1.09	b	Lake — Okeechobee
1.010	g	Swanee — River
1.011	f	mocking — bird

1.012	yes
1.013	no
1.014	yes
1.015	yes
1.016	yes
1.017	no
1.018	no
1.019	yes
1.020	yes
1.021	yes

Self Test 2

2.01	no	
2.02	no	
2.03	yes	
2.04	no	
2.05	yes	
2.06	yes	
2.07	yes	
2.08	no	
2.09	yes	
2.010	yes	
2.011	c	rocket — missile
2.012	e	swamp — Everglades
2.013	f	scientist — Dr. Goddard
2.014	g	citrus fruit — oranges
2.015	a	satellite — Sputnik
2.016	d	Lake — Okeechobee
2.017	b	Florida — Sunshine State
2.018	satellite	
2.019	Sputnik	
2.020	launched	
2.021	birds	

2.022 scientists

2.023 earth

2.024 fireworks

2.025 Swanee

2.026 dangerous

2.027 Florida

2.028 Any order:

    a.   alligators

    b.   birds

    c.   fish, snakes

2.029 Any order:

    a.   gantry operator

    b.   truck driver

    c.   weatherman or scientists, engineers, technicians, builders

2.030 Either order:

    a.   fireworks

    b.   bombs or launching satellites, space travel

2.031 Example:

A satellite is anything that travels in a

path around something else.

2.032 Either order:

    a.   Dr. Goddard

    b.   Sir Isaac Newton

2.033 Sir Isaac Newton explained how and why a rocket works.

2.034 Example:

Dr. Goddard studied rockets and space travel.

2.035 Either order:

    a.   rockets

    b.   antennas, gantry tower, or trucks

2.036 Either order:

    a.   Everglades National Park

    b.   John F. Kennedy Space Center Cape Canaveral, or Lake Okeechobee

Self Test 3

3.01 c

3.02 f

3.03 d

3.04 e

3.05 a

3.06 b

3.07 g

3.08 state

3.09 away

3.010 astronaut

3.011 God

3.012 dust

3.013 Atlantic

3.014 citrus

3.015 creator

3.016 monsters

3.017 pictures

3.018 weather

3.019 Bible

3.020 center

3.021 yes

3.022 no

3.023 no

3.024 yes

3.025 no

3.026 no

3.027 no

3.028 yes

3.029 Example:

because Florida has nice weather and is near the ocean

3.030 "That's one small step for man, one giant leap for mankind."

3.031 He flew the command ship.

3.032 Example:

I would like to be a technician and watch the rockets on the screens.

3.033 Any order:

    a   Shepard

    b.   Glenn or Aldrin, Armstrong, Chaffee, Collins, Grissom, White

3.034 Example:

    a.   orange trees

    b.   or lakes, beaches, rockets, alligators, birds, fish

Self Test 1

1.01	false	1.012	All-American Canal
1.02	true	1.013	fall
1.03	false	1.014	flour
1.04	false	1.015	vegetables
1.05	true	1.016	Lebanon — Kansas
1.06	false	1.017	Seattle — Washington
1.07	true	1.018	Los Angeles — California
1.08	false	1.019	Topeka — Kansas
1.09	Kansas	1.020	Sacramento — California
1.010	Kansas	1.021	Olympia — Washington
1.011	orchards		

Self Test 2

2.01	Kansas	2.016	Texas — Austin
2.02	Atlantic	2.017	Pennsylvania — Harrisburg
2.03	Kansas or Lebanon, Kansas	2.018	year-round
2.04	Pennsylvania	2.019	irrigate
2.05	Pacific	2.020	fall
2.06	Maine	2.021	herring
2.07	Oregon	2.022	Douglas fir
2.08	Oregon	2.023	coal
2.09	Texas	2.024	resource
2.010	Maine	2.025	ranches
2.011	Oregon — Salem	2.026	irrigate
2.012	Washington — Olympia	2.027	hides
2.013	Kansas — Topeka	2.028	replanted
2.014	Maine — Augusta	2.029	buoys
2.015	California — Sacramento	2.030	fuel

Self Test 3

3.01   Kansas — wheat

3.02   Maine — lobster

3.03   Washington — apples

3.04   Oregon — lumber business

3.05   Texas — cattle

3.06   Pennsylvania — coal

3.07   California — truck farming

3.08   Florida — space

3.09   Michigan — manufacturing

3.010 good soil

3.011 mill

3.012 the sunshine

3.013 cars

3.014 hail

3.015 John F. Kennedy Space Center

3.016 Michigan

3.017 apple blossoms

3.018 irrigation

3.019 ranch

3.020 coal

3.021 space traveler

3.022 in factories

3.023 farming

3.024 cereals

3.025 Oregon

3.026 Michigan

3.027 western

3.028 lumberjack — trees

3.029 astronaut — space

3.030 rancher — cattle

3.031 miner — coal

3.032 farmer — wheat

Notes

History & Geography 301
LIFEPAC Test

1. false
2. true
3. false
4. true
5. true
6. true
7. false
8. true
9. true
10. true
11. stone
12. sale
13. pots
14. Iowa
15. uncle

16. bait
17. state
18. sardines
19. town
20. boat
21. b.   X   fish
22. a.   X   twelve inches long
23. a.   X   sale
24. c.   X   fish
25. trap
26. fog
27. net
28. quarry
29. lobsters

History & Geography 302
LIFEPAC Test

1. true
2. false
3. true
4. true
5. false
6. true
7. true
8. false
9. false
10. false
11. X   a. winter wheat
12. X   c. soil and grass
13. X   b. Indian
14. X   c. plowed

15. X   c. Topeka
16. X   c. preserves
17. X   b. dry weather
18. X   b. wheat
19. X   c. Dodge City
20. X   c. grasshoppers
21. preserves
22. elevators
23. flour
24. dugouts
25. strip mining
26. There was not enough wood in Kansas.
27. Rain and hailstorms
28. They can destroy a wheat crop.

History & Geography 303
LIFEPAC Test

1. true
2. false
3. true
4. true
5. false
6. true
7. false
8. true
9. false
10. false
11. many waters
12. Big Chief
13. dam
14. river
15. north of Washington
16. mountains

17. cut

Any order:

18. washed
19. rinsed
20. polished
21. sorted
22. graded
23. packed
24. pruners
25. pickers
26. sorters
27. trimmers
28. washers-rinsers
29. packers
30. pollen painters

History & Geography 304
LIFEPAC Test

1. no
2. yes
3. yes
4. yes
5. no
6. yes
7. yes
8. no
9. yes
10. no
11. logging show
12. drying

13. break up a log jam
14. Timber
15. rings
16. nursery
17. chemicals
18. weather
19. smoke jumper
20. volcano
21. tree spotter
22. ape
23. truck
24. dynamite

25. conifer
    Examples:
26. pencil
27. desk
28. table
29. house
30. chair

History & Geography 305
LIFEPAC Test

1. Mexico
2. Jesus
3. California
4. tar
5. swallows
6. Sutter's Mill
7. community
8. sequoia trees
9. thank you
10. good morning
11. priest
12. pulling little plants
13. The Place of Gold
14. no
15. yes
16. no
17. yes
18. yes
19. yes
20. yes
21. tar pits
22. gold
23. irrigation, truck farms, carrots, lettuce
24. swallows, mission
25. cable car, Chinatown
26. capital
27. zoo
28. vegetables
29. Pacific
30. to use what the other makes

History & Geography 306
LIFEPAC Test

1. brand
2. Any order:
   a. milk
   b. meat
   c. hides
3. cities
4. cattle
5. trucks
6. herd
7. Mexico
8. panhandle
9. ranch
10. Texarkana
11. hard

12. <u>rain</u>
13. <u>oil</u>
14. <u>cattle</u>
15. <u>Indians</u>
16. <u>Dallas and Fort Worth</u>
17. no
18. no
19. yes
20. yes
21. no
22. yes
23. no
24. yes
25. yes
26. no
27. yes

28. yes
29. no
30. ~~funny~~
31. ~~Wrangler~~
32. ~~by plane~~
33. ~~clerk~~
34. ~~eat cake~~
35. blue pants — worn around the neck
36. outrider — rode ahead
37. bunkhouse — cowboy house
38. Rio Grande — river
39. mouth — where river goes into large body of water
40. scarf — blue jeans

History & Geography 307
LIFEPAC Test

1. fuel
2. explosives
3. by-product
4. swamp
5. work
6. energy
7. props
8. gas
9. town
10. 3
11. 2
12. 1
13. 4

14. (a great man in America's history)
15. (energy)
16. (fairly)
17. (strip mining)
18. (Philadelphia)
19. (machines)
20. (God)
21. true
22. true
23. false
24. true
25. false

History & Geography 308
LIFEPAC Test

1.   true
2.   false
3.   false
4.   true
5.   false
6.   true
7.   false
8.   true
9.   false
10. true
11. g. upper peninsula
12. h. Detroit
13. e. inspector
14. i or h. Ford Motor Plant
15. a. Lake Michigan
16. b. passenger pigeon
17. c. Martha-Mary Church
18. j. "Horseless Carriage"
19. d. tulip festival
20. f. "Big Mac"

a. Great Lake
b. extinct
c. in Greenfield village
d. Holland, Michigan
e. checks things
f. Large suspension bridge
g. shaped like a bird
h. known for making automobiles
i. a factory
j. name for a car

21. manufactures
22. cereal
23. license
24. automobile
25. hymn
26. President
27. quickly
28. wrong
29. God
30. wildlife
31. tourists
32. Any order:
   a.   water
   b.   forests
   c.   minerals
   d.   wildlife
   e.   fur
33. Example: I would like to visit Greenfield Village because there are so many interesting historic buildings to see.

History & Geography 309
LIFEPAC Test

1.   Florida
2.   Sunshine
3.   Gateway
4.   Everglades
5.   scientist
6.   satellite
7.   "birds"
8.   Canaveral
9.   astronaut
10. capsule
11. yes
12. no
13. no
14. yes

15. no

16. yes

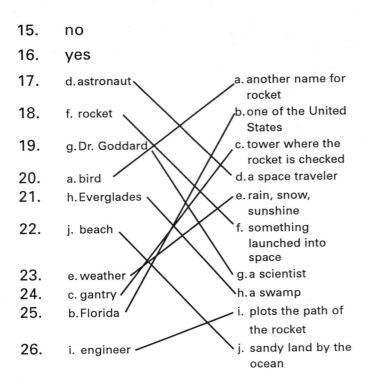

17. d. astronaut   a. another name for rocket
18. f. rocket   b. one of the United States
19. g. Dr. Goddard   c. tower where the rocket is checked
20. a. bird   d. a space traveler
21. h. Everglades   e. rain, snow, sunshine
22. j. beach   f. something launched into space
23. e. weather   g. a scientist
24. c. gantry   h. a swamp
25. b. Florida   i. plots the path of the rocket
26. i. engineer   j. sandy land by the ocean

History & Geography 310
LIFEPAC Test

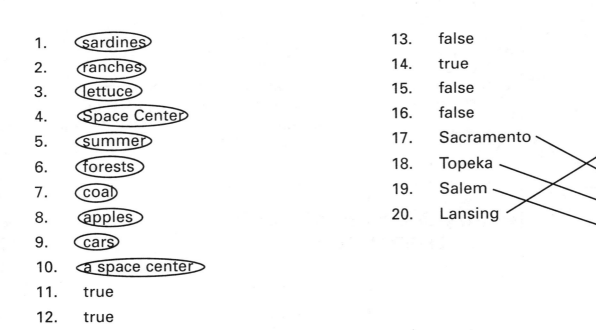

1. sardines
2. ranches
3. lettuce
4. Space Center
5. summer
6. forests
7. coal
8. apples
9. cars
10. a space center
11. true
12. true

13. false
14. true
15. false
16. false
17. Sacramento   Michigan
18. Topeka   Florida
19. Salem   California
20. Lansing   Kansas
                     Oregon